**HOW
BLACK PEOPLE
OVERCAME
FIFTY YEARS
OF REPRESSION
IN BRITAIN
1945-1995
(Volume One: 1945-1975)**

By The Same Author:

- BRITAIN, THE BLACK MAN AND THE FUTURE;

- BLACK YOUTH AND THE SURVIVAL GAME IN
  BRITAIN;

- A MOVEMENT FOR CHANGE; AND

- PAN EUROPEANISM AND RACISM

How Black People Overcame Fifty Years of Repression in Britain

Volume One: 1945-1975

By

Vince Hines

Published by Zulu Publications

First published 1998

Published by:

Zulu Publications
150 Townmead Road
London
SW6 2RA
Tel/Fax: +44 (0)171 384 2876
E-mail: zulu@ubol.com

**Strength
Of
The Oppressed**

We are not afraid !

**At times, the greatest
Strength of the oppressed
Is their oppression.**

**We are now facing the world
Of oppression together
And we shall survive.**

**We are making demands
And winning the battle
For freedom, equality and justice**

**Stand firm always
Even in times
Of grave difficulties.
Therein lies our strength.**

Now is our time !

Vince Hines

THE AUTHOR

Vince Hines is the National Director of the Black European Community Development Federation (BECDF), which incorporated the National Federation Of Self-Help Organisations, based in the United Kingdom.

He was born 19th July, 1942, St. Ann's Bay, Jamaica, West Indies, the son of Ivy and Thomas. He shares similar birth place with the Pan-Africanist and Visionary, Marcus Mosiah Garvey, 1887-1940. Vince Hines did his general education at the St Ann's Bay Secondary Modern.

He immigrated to England in May 1961 and joined his father, Thomas, a Civil Engineer in London. One month later, he joined the Royal Air Force (RAF), and after three months' military induction training, he joined the RAF Central School of Navigation. After the successful completion of his Course, he joined the RAF Air Traffic Control Services.

He served five years in the RAF, during which he continued his education at the RAF School of Education and through correspondence courses. He travelled widely, going to the Middle and Far East, 1963-65.

He was demobilised from the RAF in 1966 and joined the British Civil Service, the Department of Employment and Productivity, in Whitehall later that year. After a year in the Civil Service, he left and attended the City of London College, where he studied Economics and Politics. Subsequently, he studied Journalism at the London School of Journalism.

In 1971 he joined Fleet Street as a trained journalist. He became a member of the National Union of Journalists (NUJ) and contributed to the *Guardian, Mirror, Sun, Time*

Out, Race Today, Socialist Worker, Ink, International Times (IT), Seven Day, West Indian Digest, West Indian World, Caribbean Post, West Indian Voice, among others. He joined BBC Radio as a Reporter 1972-73, and made a number of television broadcasts.

He contributed extensively to charitable and voluntary work in the African and Caribbean Community. He co-founded the Council For Afro-Asian Peoples (CAAP) and became its first President in 1969-1971.

He founded and directed the Dashiki Council - a charitable body and one of the first independent Black-managed self-help organisations in Britain for multi-deprived and homeless youngsters - between 1972-75. Based on the Dashiki model, a network of Black-managed self-help, social and welfare projects was generated through England and Wales, which benefited members of the African, African Caribbean, Asian and Caucasian Communities.

In 1975 a number of well-known and highly respected men and women came together and formed an education charity, registered at the Charity Commission, called The Vince Hines Foundation, in recognition of the important work Vince Hines has been doing in the Community. Over the twenty three years of its work in the Community, the Foundation had helped over sixteen thousand members of the community in the field of education, training, social, welfare, legal and housing matters. Vince Hines is a Trustee of the Foundation.

He is author of: *Britain, The Black Man And The Future; Black Youth And The Survival Game In Britain; A Movement For Change And Pan Europeanism And Racism. He edited "Self-Help News",* a national newspaper circulated within the Self-Help Movement in Britain 1980-90 and *"The Advocate"* Magazine, 1993 - 1997.

In 1977 he gained a Doctorate in Social Science from the Ministerial Academy, a USA Academic Establishment with Annex in London. He previously held a Master's degree.

Vince Hines is co-founder of Britain's largest Black-managed National umbrella Organisation, The National Federation of Self-Help Organisations and its first Chairperson during 1975-85. He was Chairperson of the Confederation of African Nationals and Descendants, 1991-94 and Chairperson, 1990-1998, of The Standing Conference of African And Asian Peoples In Europe, set up in 1990 at Liverpool's historic African-Asian Conference, 14,15 and 16 September, 1990.

He is BECDF representative on the Local Government Association's Community Development Forum, based in London, and a representative at the Standing Conference For Community Development, based in Sheffield

Dr Hines is Founder and a Trustee of the African And Caribbean Institute For Community Education (UK) and a member of East London University's *Afrika (Africa) Studies Centre* Steering Committee and Academic Sub-Committee.

Zulu Publications
March, 1998

Dedication

This work is dedicated to ALL those who are learning and gaining confidence in themselves to overcome the hypnosis of deception and deceit

Thank You

Thank you Horace M. Lashley, Alma Smith, Dr Osakwe Osifo, Dr (Mrs) Biola Molokwu, Callistus Igboanugo and Clifford Parris for taking the time to read the early drafts of the manuscript of this work, and thanks to all those whose names have not appeared here for your dedicated support over the years. Yours have been equally important as those whose names are mentioned.

"And this, O men of Athens, is the truth and the whole truth; I have concealed nothing, I have dissembled nothing.

And yet I feel sure that my plainness of speech is fanning their hatred of me, and what is their hatred of me, but a proof that I am speaking the truth."

Socrates in the Dialogues of Plato

Contents

How
Black People
Overcame
Fifty Years
Of Repression
In Britain
1945-1995
(Volume One: 1945-1975)

Vince Hines

1.   Introduction

THEY CAME AND BUILT BRITAIN'S war torn
economy...British firms actively recruited workers from
the Commonwealth and Colonies, during the 1950s, 60s
and 70s, including British Transport[1] and the National
Health Service... Government ministers at the time
described West Indian immigrants as 'model citizens.'

Sir Winston Churchill told the people in the Caribbean
after World War II, "The Mother Country needs you.
Come and help rebuild her. Think British. Be British. You
are British."[2] It was believed that Churchill made that
speech in light of the fact that large numbers of West
Indian men of African origins were contracted by the
USA Government as farm labourers in the Southern
States. The people in the Caribbean believed Churchill.

By 22 June, 1948, the *Empire Windrush* brought to
Tilbury Docks 492 Jamaicans to help Britain and gain a
higher standard of living for themselves and their
families. The *Empire Windrush* was an historic
symbolism, which pioneered the way for other Shipping

Liners like *Orbita, Reina del Pacifico and Georgic to start transporting a steady stream of West Indian immigrants to England.* By the summer of 1949, Britain received her first thousand West Indian immigrants. Ten years later, according to Peter Fryers, in his Book, *STAYING POWER - The History of Black People In Britain**, 125,000 West Indians arrived in England, since the end of World War II. This compared with 55,000 Indians and Pakistanis for the same period.

The British West Indies were those chain of islands situated between North and South America, including Guyana, south of the islands and north of the South American Continent. Many of these islands were -and still are - holiday havens for the wealthy from the industrialised countries. The rich came because of the islands' warm and pleasant weather and friendly people.

Prime Minister Churchill, in making his pitch for the West Indians to come to 'Mother' Britain was addressing people mostly of African origins, who were made to live and work as slaves during the 16th to 19th century, by the ancestors of many of the very same type of people whom Winston Churchill was representing. The African people were brought in chains to the Caribbean islands to work on British (White) sugar plantations. Other people from India and China made their homes on the islands subsequently.

Those from India were contracted by the plantation owners as indentured labourers. The Indian and Chinese were not slaves; but cheap labour. The Caribs and Arawaks had long populated the islands. There were attempts by the Whites to make the Arawaks and Caribs slaves, but the natives could not cope with the very hard work imposed and died. Others died of the new diseases which arrived from Europe - small pox, cholera and

---

* Published by Pluto Press, London 1984 and 1989.

similar diseases among the Caucasians. A melting pot of sorts developed in the Caribbean during the past one hundred years among the people of colour.

In a recent work by Alma Smith,[3] freelance researcher, she stated "most of the people are farmers or fishermen, and in spite of poor wages, high unemployment and the resulting low standard of living on many of the Islands, the people generally adopted a fairly light-hearted attitude towards life. Most have a strong religious background, and this tradition has continued with the migrants who travelled to the United Kingdom ."

As a result of Churchill's invitation, the 1948 British Nationality Act provided British citizenship to the people from the British Commonwealth and Colonies, giving a right to enter, reside and work in Britain indefinitely. Evidently, the West Indies fielded the majority[4] of immigrants to Britain during the 1950s and 60s.

After they had arrived in Britain and gave their all, members of the Black - African and African Caribbean - Communities were often projected by sections of the media as 'problems', associated with drugs, lawlessness, under achievements and a 'drain' on the social fabric of society.

Before the *Empire Windrush* Black people from the British Commonwealth fought side by side British and allied troops in Europe, during 1939 and 1945 War, the aim of which was to rid Europe of racism and fascism. Liberation came in 1945, but by 1955, it was as though there was no liberation. Racism and fascism of sorts were real to Black ex-servicemen and women, their relatives and country men and women who were joining them in Britain.

They were greeted by the White 'liberated' with 'no coloured', 'no dogs', 'no Irish', when many Black people sought the essential things of life - housing, jobs, food and clothing, to sustain independent living in England. Members of White Britain were to enjoy the fruits of 'liberation', but not members of the Black immigrant community, invitees of the British Government. The opportunity to develop good community and race relations was missed, and what followed shaped the future of race relations in Britain. The rejection of Black people, began the process of White Britain's social construction of a *black monster*. Fifty years later, the end results of that construction are revealed as they haunt a multi-cultural Britain.

In reality, that type of social construction suits those who had a long term hidden agenda to frustrate the real aspirations and inevitable upward mobile movement of Black people, in Europe and elsewhere.

The British National Health Service and transport system could not have functioned efficiently without the support of Black nurses, midwives, doctors bus drivers and conductors.

Winston Churchill, Prime Minister, sought ways of keeping Black people out of the Home Civil Service. Mr R.A. Butler was asked by Sir Winston Churchill's Cabinet in 1954 to produce a report on ways of stopping Black people getting jobs in the Civil Service.

The request to Butler, who, as Chancellor of the Exchequer, was responsible for Civil Service matters, reflected the deep anxiety of Churchill's Government's two-face policy on immigration from the West Indies and West Africa.

In the late autumn of 1954 the Home Office produced figures showing that immigration from the West Indies had increased to 10,000 a year. According to the official minutes at the time, the Cabinet agonised over several sessions, discussing new rules for deporting Black people convicted of offences or those who were 'a charge on public funds'.

The Cabinet minutes recorded Prime Minister Churchill to have said: "The rapid improvement of communications was likely to lead to a continuing increase in the numbers of coloured people coming to this country, and their presence here would sooner or later come to be resented by large sections of the British people,". Trouble spots mentioned were Manchester and Paddington, London. The issue was seen by the Cabinet as non-partisan.

The 'worries' of Labour MPs were cited and Churchill said he would consult Clement Attlee, Leader of the Opposition, on necessary measures. Lord Swinton, Secretary for Commonwealth Relations, wanted a policy of welcoming the comparatively few "good young" Canadians or New Zealanders (both white skin people) who wished to work in Britain, and legislation to restrict West Indians and West Africans was called for urgently.

Cabinet papers for 1954 declassified on 19 October, 1985 and available for public view at the Public Record Office at Kew showed how even before Britain acquired significant numbers of non-white inhabitants, public officials were worried about the social effects.

The Home Secretary, Gwllym Lloyd-George, predicted ominously that foreign ship-owners would soon cash in by speeding up the flow of West Indians and West Africans to Britain. It was not until eight years after Churchill Cabinet raised the spectre of immigration controls, Mr Harold Macmillan's Conservative Government introduced in 1962 Britain's first immigration Act. By then mass immigration had increased the number of Black people living in Britain considerably.

Based on the above background to government and official thinking during the 1950s and 60s, the stage was set for a period of considerable social repression of Black people by the State. Nearly all social, economic and political considerations which followed had their roots in the foundation, which was laid by the Churchill's Administration. What was being said to the Black immigrants, by the government and large numbers of the population was: 'cheap labour yes - social mobility no'. That message was clearly understood by the White indigenous majority population, from which members of the British police forces were recruited. From here on social repression against Black people in Britain seemed to have been the order of the decades.

As a response, the Black Community built up a unique community development infrastructure in Britain, during 1945-1995, of which members of that Community must celebrate.

That was done through *self-help* and community organisations, including supplementary schools, community businesses and credit unions. This is Volume One of two volumes, detailing some experiences and survival tactics of Black people, which focussed primarily on people of African descents, as they had the greater brunt of social repression during the period being assessed. Volume One will focus on 1945 to 1975 and Volume Two on 1976 to 1995.

2. Decision To Come To Britain 1945-1975

BLACK PEOPLE sacrificed many lives for 'mother' Britain during the 1939-45 War, when the cream, the youth of the Commonwealth, came and fought side by side with British troops to defeat fascism in Europe.

Black men and women, particularly from the Caribbean, served in the British Navy, Army and Air Force, as enlisted men and officers. Those - ordinary Black men, women and children - in the Caribbean and other parts of the British Commonwealth, who did not travel to Britain, contributed to the war efforts by growing and shipping foods to the British people to keep them fed, during the difficult times of the war.

Britain did not pay market rate for the foods she received, because she could not pay. There was no question of 'market forces' then. The foods were not shipped to Germany, Italy or Japan. Only to Britain - 'Mother Britain'.

Then, Black people in the British colonies were heroes to the British media and White Britain. The line was clearly drawn, Black sailors, soldiers and airmen, fighters at the time, were told by the British government, and they believed it, that they were fighting for Britain, and once fascism and anti-Semitism were defeated, Black service men and women felt assured that their children and grand children would have earned the rights to the benefits of a 'liberated' Britain. 'Rule Britannia - let the bells of freedom ring loud and clear'.

The war ended and the hugs and kisses faded, replaced by racial discrimination, insults and institutionalised

20

racism. British public seemed to have forgotten the citations of their Black war heroes and the contributions Black people in the colonies made to feed and liberate Britannia.

West Indian ex-servicemen and women recalled that same members of the White Community in Britain, saying to them - 'the war is over - when are you going home ?'. The Black ex-servicemen and women said that they often replied that they too fought and were entitled to their bit of freedom in Britain as well as other loyal citizens.

Today, very few post war and contemporary children know of the contributions Black people made to the war efforts. On grand occasions, such as the Remembrance Day Celebration at the Cenotaph, in Whitehall Central London, and elsewhere in Britain, it is a rarity to see Black ex-servicemen and women marching with their White colleagues. This event is televised throughout the nation. This is community education.

The ordinary citizens - Black and White - should be forgiven to conclude that Black people made no contribution to Britain's war efforts, and that they had nothing to commemorate. This is a deliberate distortion, by implication, of history, by the leaders of our British Establishment.

Where is the Royal British Legion embrace, overt or covert, which commemorates the memory of fallen Black servicemen and women ? Europe's wars - I and II, were not the Blackman's wars. At the time, Black people were under the yoke of colonialism in the Caribbean, Africa and indeed parts of Asia, by the major players of the wars, albeit less so by Germany. Black people were involved by their colonial administrators to take sides.

The 1960s, 70s, 80s and 90s were to see the overt return of the enemies which were believed to have been defeated twenty years earlier - racism, fascism, anti-Semitism xenophobia and religious intolerance.

Today, Black ex-servicemen and women of the 1940s are grand parents, and many are still residing in Britain. They lived to witness Britain's core politics telling their grand children that they had no 'real' moral claim on Britain, and the ex-service men and women asked, 'what was the fighting about ?'

This lack of true historical focus, as it affected members of the Black Community, began during the 1950s. At the time, Britain was still having an influx of immigrants from the British Commonwealth and colonies.

Black people again responded to Britain's call for help and they came in their thousands in 1950s to help Britain, and to gain the livelihood denied them in their own countries, because of the stranglehold which Britain and other Western powers exercised over their economies, and have exercised for hundreds of years as a result of colonialism.

The vast majority of the new immigrants were strong, healthy, young men and women, who came from humble villages. They were ordinary and even simple people. They were above all sincere, religious, honest, ambitious and hard working. What was certain, they knew nothing about racial discrimination or colour bar, as they existed in Britain.

Britain's so-called right wing politicians made sure that the new comers learned quickly about racial discrimination. On the streets, White 'Teddy Boys', part of Britain's working class youth culture, which moved on later to 'Skinheads', were aggressive and anti-black mobs. Teddy Boys and Skinheads attacked Black people on the streets, simply because their skins were black. Other 1950s and 60s White youth cultures were 'Mods' (Modernist) and 'Rockers' - both were followers[1] of popular youth fashion and music style in Britain at the time, who were not pre-occupied with racial attacks on members of the immigrant community. Not all White youth cultures were hostile to the immigrants.

Black workers came to Britain for two main reasons:

a) There was a labour shortage in Britain, and industry and government went out of their way to attract Commonwealth citizens and other foreigners to come and work in Britain. The Aliens Order of 1920 was relaxed to admit foreigners under Ministry of Labour permit to work in certain industries. In 1948, the British Nationality Act gave free entry to citizens in the Black Commonwealth.   Barbados in the West Indies, for example, was a central area, where London Transport recruitment was at the highest; and

b) The centuries of British Imperialism in the British Commonwealth impoverished these countries: unemployment and poverty forced Black people to leave their homes and look for jobs in Britain.

World War II left behind a great gap in labour. Some British industries, like the car industry, were expanding and productivity could be increased either by modernising, in order that a large part of the work was automated, or by getting more labour. Getting more labour was the answer, but at the time the population rate of growth was declining. Britain had to look outside for labour supply.

---

[1] Robins, David - Tarnished Vision: Crime And Conflict In The Inner City. Glossary page 131. Published by Oxford University Press 1992.

At the time, British White workers were leaving certain industries. These were the more menial, arduous, unpleasant and low paid jobs. White workers were deserting them as other opportunities arose in this period of growth. The new arrivals lived mainly in the urban industrial areas of England: London, the South East, the West Midlands and the North.

The largest number of Black people worked in textiles: clothing; small manufacturers; plastics; foundries; metal work; transport (as railway guards, porters, bus conductors) and service industries (kitchen hands, waiters, hospital orderlies) as well as engineering and electrical goods.

The immigrants also worked in the construction industry and a few in agriculture. The British Health Service was well known for the number of Black doctors and nurses it attracted. Black people were overwhelmingly in the labourer category, the most menial and lowest paid grades.

The work involved pushing, pulling and dragging; but with the development of a continuous process of production, it became impossible to determine where traditional labouring work finished and other classification begins. In the past, for example, BMC hired Black workers, it was possible for labourers to be up-graded to semi-skilled jobs.

Night work was another labourer category that many White workers avoided. The Black workers were hired in large numbers to the northern textile factories which were manned at night almost entirely by Black workers.

Black worker got the hard and dirty jobs in the foundry and small manufacturing industries, like the North London cluster. Black workers were concentrated in small firms, which could only operate profitably with cheap labour, and where conditions were often Victorian, with 12-hour shifts, no tea breaks, no canteen and no proper ventilation.

In 1962[5], a survey showed that Black workers earned 30% less than the average for manual work in Britain. In 1966 the average earning for all male workers was £20 per week. The average pay of a Black worker in Manchester was £16-£18 (£14-£16 take home pay), that is 15-18% less than the national average. Taking income per head as the measure, in 1966 the average for a Black worker was 22% below the White population.

---

[5] Hines, V., Britain, The Black Man And The Future. Zulu Books 1972

3. Black People And Trades Unions 1960-1975

Black workers were the least likely to become members of trades union initially for the following reason:

a) The industries in which they worked were traditionally weak in trade union organisations, being very often small or with a high turnover of unskilled labour;

b) Employers in small firms were often strongly against union activities, and sacked anyone who attempted to organise;

c) Unions themselves hardly helped Black people to defend themselves and fight for their rights and they discouraged Black people when they tried to take industrial action.

However, Black workers had been organising and taking action, where they experienced inequalities at the work place. There had been hard and solid strikes in many places where there had been sufficient Black workers to make industrial action viable.

In 1965 there was a strike of Black workers in a Courtaul Mill in Preston, Lancashire. The total work force was 2,400. Two workshops consisted entirely of Black workers - 130 in all. The management and the union officials (The Transport and General Workers Union (TGWU)) argued jointly to impose on the two Black departments 1.5 times extra work for a certain bonus. The Black workers refused and held a 17-hour sit-in at the plant, which led to a strike. Their White colleagues did not come out in support.

The TGWU declared the strike 'unofficial', stigmatising it as a 'racial' strike, because only the Black workers were involved. The local trades council's secretary said at the time: "If they (the Black workers) don't like it here, there are plenty of trains, boats and planes to take them back."

The Black workers were isolated. There was little hope for victory, and after three weeks out they returned to work. The management then forced all the workers, including the Whites, who did not support the strike, to do extra work for the bonus.

There was a major strike by Black workers at Woolf's Solar Works in Southall in 1966. That was a rubber firm, employing 800 workers, and that unskilled labour force consisted of a Black majority. The Black workers tried to organise a union, which the management refused to recognise. Eventually, a union was formed, and in November 1966, a dispute over pay and working conditions led to a strike of 600 workers which lasted for six weeks.

The TGWU refused to recognise the strike and there was no strike pay. The Black Community in Southall helped the strikers with money and goods. There was a heroic effort to stay out, but without union support, workers eventually had to return to work.

On May 2, 1969, over 300 Black workers employed by P.B. Cow Industrial Rubber Company Ltd., in Streatham, South London, went on strike for the dismissal of a Black worker. The workers downed their tools and marched to the Personnel Office. The workers demanded the immediate re-instatement of the dismissed worker. After two days of militant strike, the workers forced the bosses to reinstate the sacked worker.

John Davies, 35, a Black factory worker explained at the time: "I find that being a part of a White union is only a formality at the moment. I pay my union dues and carry a union card because of the principle. I haven't had the sort of support from the union that I would like".

John continued: "I had a dispute with my boss recently and I asked a White Shop Steward for support. He made all sorts of excuses and in the end I had to forget the whole idea of the dispute."

Carl, 45, a Black Ticket Collector with British Rails, earning £16.50p per week - take home pay £11, rent £5.75p, plus £1 for electricity and gas - lived in Paddington, West London with a wife and two children.

Carl: "I am pessimistic about the future for the Black working class under the present British system. I don't think that the bosses will give anything unless they are forced to. I think that the poor, Black and White, accept too much shit.

"We should protest strongly. Some people think that if they win the pools, or the dogs and horses, everything will be all right - but everybody can't win," Carl concluded.

In those cases where members of the Asian Community made up the majority of workers in the affected department, the Asian workers took the initiatives on strike action, and people of African origins gave support. Historical photographs, which recorded the strikes, showed African and Asian workers standing side by side in solidarity.

The Black Trade Unionists Solidarity Movement - in which Bernie Grant, later to become the Labour Party Member of Parliament, played a leading role, as a response to the failure of the wider trades union movement in looking after the interest of their Black members, during the late 1970s and 1980s.

4. Black Women In The Front Line Of Struggle 1950-1975

During the 1960s, 89% of Black women go out to work in Britain, as compared with 49% of White women. Black women entered factories, transport, catering, health and commerce, and were divided into two groups: the older ones tended to enter factories, transport and catering; the younger ones entered nursing and commerce, partly because they had a higher standard of education.

Whatever their education, Black women came heavily under the capitalist hammer at the time. A large number of women did night cleaning for ridiculously low wages - £10 weekly for work done from 10pm to 6am.

Mrs Sharon Maxim, 35, a Catering Assistant, came from Antigua in 1956. She lived in Notting Hill Gate. She had three children living in a poor run-down house near a slum clearance area for which she paid £5 per week for two rooms. She shared a cooker with five other tenants and toilet with seven - no bathroom. The rooms were damp, which meant the paraffin heaters were constantly in use during the winter months to provide adequate heating, thus increased fire risk. Central heating in working class homes - Black and White - was unheard of during the early 1960s. Coal and gas fires and paraffin heaters were used to heat homes.

Sharon explained: " I don't care so much for myself but the children. I always dread the winter and the heater. So many Black people die in fires during the winter time. I look for a new place to live time and time again, but I can't find one.

30

"My biggest problem is finding nurseries for the children. The local one always seem to get full up, and people have to put their names on a long waiting list. I have to find daily minders, and they are very hard to find. I found one recently and she charged me £3 per week from 8a.m. to 6 p.m. daily. There should be more nurseries for children," Sharon concluded.

However, those Black women who had most of their education in Britain and knew how to operate the system, were more articulate and socially conscious about their position in British society.

British hospitals would probably not operate effectively without the Black immigrants. In fact, without the windfall of Black doctors, nurses and midwives in the 1960s in the National Health Service, the health authorities would have had to reduce quite severely the number of patients the Health Service treated. The influx of Black people meant that the Community had a lucky escape from the logical consequences of its own negligence in social planning.

Jenny, a 25-year old Black nurse, arrived in Britain five years earlier. She lived in Islington and was then working in Mile End Hospital in North London. Jenny explained: "I don't think that many people know this, but in the hospitals the Black and White nurses are separated.

"Why this happens I don't know. I find that when I am with a White nurse in the wards, five minutes later, when we meet in the canteen, she refuses to speak to me. She behaves as if we had never met. I felt sad when I first experienced that sort of thing - that was during my training five years ago. Now I am used to it, but I don't understand it. In a way, I was lucky, compared with some Black girls, who recently arrived in Britain to do nursing - many were accepted to do student nursing, but when they arrived, even though they had the necessary qualifications, they found that the Matron made them worked as auxiliary nurses.

"After that, the Black girls probably go on to a proper nursing course. I think that our girls are being used. I hardly ever see White girls doing auxiliary nursing. Auxiliary nurses worked as cleaners and received no training. It's hypocrisy to tell students that they will be trained as nurses when what is meant was that they would be required as labourers." Jenny said.

Jenny continued; "When I became a nurse, I just wanted to keep people alive - Black and White people. It's either I like it or I don't like it. I don't think of prejudices. When I am nursing, I see the patients as sick people I must get well. Of course some White patients sometimes abused me. I can remember one White patient telling me not to touch him with my black hands, and I replied that it was a pleasure not to touch him with these beautiful hands." Jenny maintained that Black nurses, like all nurses, were dissatisfied with pay and working conditions.

Subsequently, the Jamaican Nurses' Association (UK) was formed to give support to Black nurses.

Commerce was another attraction for Black women. Over 80% of second generation British Black people of African descents entered this field and became typists, clerk and secretaries. They were not readily offered jobs. In fact, they were more likely to be refused jobs than the Black women who entered the factories, transport and catering.

Sonya, 20, lived in Lewisham, South East London, in 1972. She was a trained secretary to a White Executive of a well-known company in London.

Sonya said: "Before I got this job, I attended interviews following interviews. I almost gave up and tried for a job on the buses. Somehow my luck changed and I got the job. I found that some White employers didn't like my looking different. My White boss sometimes asked why I was wearing my hair like that, [an Afro-hair style] and I told him that it was a fashion. I didn't think that he would have understood if I had told him that it was a cultural change."

Sonya was asked what she thought of western society establishing the White woman as the symbol of beauty. "To be quite truthful," said Sonya, "I am not concerned with the White woman and her beauty. We Black women have an identity of our own, and we should not hide it.

"As a Black woman, I have began to question my own motives and goals concerning my personal life and the life of my people. We have great responsibilities as far as our men, our children and our survival are concerned.

"I think that the first of our responsibilities is to define ourselves. We as Black women must be aware of our abilities and shortcomings. We cannot relate to others effectively if we are not aware of what we are about.

"A Black women has to decide how 'black' she wants to be. When refer to blackness, I do not only mean the physical manifestations of the new Black culture. I also mean a mental condition, an awareness of the place we occupy in the society and what we must do for our continued existence. Our degree of blackness will determine how well we relate to other people, Black and White people.

"If we are 'militant' we may go to jail; if we are complacent, White society may find us ripe for co-option and pseudo-assimilation, thus making us lose sight of our own goals. It is important to have a code that represents our beliefs and we can only do this if we fully understand ourselves.

"The Black woman must consider her involvement with her Black people as a group, and try to further the collective goal of nationhood. We must begin in our own homes to build a cohesive nation of Black people, and this responsibility falls chiefly on the Black woman.

"In short, the Black woman must complement her man and help him to realise his own potentials. This doesn't mean she got to walk four steps behind him. She must walk at his side and they must work together. She must also educate her children in Black awareness and equip them for survival in this hostile environment. At the same time, she must not lose sight of her own interest and conditions. The Black woman must be a revolutionary in her creative thinking. She must revolutionise herself, then her family and eventually all Black People," Soyna concluded.

5. Black People And Housing In Britain 1950 - 1975

Many White shop keepers, landlords, employers, displayed prominent signs: ' No Children'. 'No Irish, No dogs, No coloured or N.C.P - means No Coloured Person' for jobs. In effect, Black people were not to be able to shop and eat, not to be able to live anywhere, except on the streets, and in many cases, no jobs were to be offered.

The proliferation of housing associations in the mid 1960s, and 1970s under the Industrial and Provident Society, brought with it social housing and gas central heating, in response to a television programme, *"Cathy Come Home",* which featured very bad housing conditions for a White family. The Notting Hill Housing Trust (NHHT), founded by Reverend Bruce Kenrick, White Minister, began in 1965. NHHT was a multi-racial initiative for homeless families. Later, SELTER, a campaigning pressure group for the homeless, was also formed by Bruce Kenrick, based in London.

The Housing Association Movement, led by the National Federation of Housing Association, White governed, brought with it affordable rented homes for people in housing needs. This Movement was later to become a major player in Britain's social housing, from which thousands of Black people would benefit as managers and users.

Meanwhile, until the future arrived, the Black immigrants found it very difficult to get accommodation during the 1960s and 70s. Everyone with children knows that as housing needs increase, the ability to satisfy those needs decreases.

A large family, another child coming, the older ones growing up, are the very reason that the needs are never satisfied. The greater one's need for housing, the more impossible to get it.

A loan was difficult to come by, since building societies' managers judged their applicant's status/income before they decide to give a loan. Building societies would not look at an applicant if his[1] income was below a certain level, and the majority of Black workers' income was well below that level.

Local government housing did not help much, since most councils had massive waiting lists, which discriminated against anyone born overseas. The majority of those Black applicants who managed to get council houses found that they were given old terrace houses, in or near slum clearance areas.

That was not to say that Black people were not housed in modern council accommodation. Lambeth Council was known for its liberal 'first come first served' attitude, but Lambeth was the exception to the current attitudes of other local authorities. The London County Council (LCC), later called, the Greater London Council (GLC), was a major housing provider.

Black people who had not managed to get council houses were forced to live in private rented rooms, paying exorbitant rents for space in houses, which should have been demolished ten, twenty years before. A walk along Railton Road, Brixton, South London, Moss

---

[1] The normal convention was that financial institutions dealt with the male of the household and not the female in these matters, at this juncture of Britain's social and economic history.

Manchester, Tiger Bay, Cardiff, South Wales and Glasgow ghettos were no exception, would bring home the truth of housing dilapidation at the time.

One did not need more than an average imagination to feel the pain, misery and tension that a Black and a White family felt, living, eating and sleeping in damp, sparsely furnished rooms, sharing cookers, water taps and lavatories, with other families.

Peter Walker, the Conservative Minister of Housing in 1970, emerged from two Brixton houses "appalled" by the conditions to which Black residents were subjected: "All I can do is express my complete disgust for any human being who exploits another human being in this way. I can think of no greater evil," he said and went back to Whitehall, having finally realised that there were houses where 32 people shared a single lavatory.

The Rose Report, 'Colour And Citizenship', found that Black residents were several times more likely than Whites to have to live in bad housing, one reason being that their jobs and their children tied them to the cities.

There was a natural housing shortage in Britain at the time, and even the average White citizen experienced difficulty in finding suitable housing. But Black people's situation was aggravated by the indisputable colour discrimination which operated in the housing market.

There had been examples where some Black residents slept on one bed in shifts. One shift worked in the factories by night and the other by day. The bed was continually occupied.

The good thing which came out of all this was that Black people were forced to own their own homes. The 1960s, 70s and 80s saw a high proportion of Black people owning their own homes in England.

In Central Birmingham, for example, as many as 56% of Black families were owner-occupiers, this compared with a rate of 30% owner-occupiers for White families in that area. That was African Caribbean self-help at its best.

Black home buyers were at the mercy of unscrupulous White estate agents. Black buyers had to pay twice the market value for their homes, and much of the loans on offer came from private money lenders - Rachmanits.

Black people set up credit unions, which helped towards the purchase of freehold property. The immigrants introduced a type of community savings called 'partner', where a number of friends and colleagues clubbed together and pooled their capital and allowed each member of the group to have the pooled cash in turns.

This ready cash, help participants to purchase what they needed at the time, or even pay towards getting family members and relatives, left behind in the Caribbean, to England.

By 1965, Britain passed her first Race relations Act, followed by similar acts in 1968 and 1976, which outlawed racial discrimination in jobs, housing and sales of goods and services. The Rent Act of 1965 also came into forced which gave some protection to tenants from the exploits of unreasonable landlords.

6. Black Children, Their Education And The Birth Of The Supplementary Education Movement In Britain 1960-1975

Most of the immigrants from Africa at the time were students, 'who did not come to Britain to settle'. 'West Indians' were generally settlers who 'came home to Mother Britain and found that 'Mother' rejected them, when in reality, Britain never believed that Black People were ever her children.

The Majority of Black immigrants started a family in Britain. Those who had a family before they came, sent for them on their arrival. As a result, there was a large number of Black youth in Britain during 1960s, 70s,and 80s.

Black children were generally found in poor quality schools and a large number were placed wrongly in educational sub-normal classes.

Bernard Coard, born in Jamaica, a Black school teacher, in Britain, wrote in his book, "HOW THE WEST INDIAN CHILD IS MADE EDUCATIONALLY SUB-NORMAL IN THE BRITISH SCHOOL SYSTEM" (Published by New Beacon Books, 1971): "An inner London Education Authority report entitled 'The Education of Immigrant Pupils In Special Schools For Educationally Sub-Normal Children' (ILEA657) reveals that five of their secondary ESN schools had more than 30% immigrants at the time of their survey in 1967. By January 1968, one of the school had 60% immigrant children.

"In the ILEA's ESN (Special) Day Schools, over 28% of all the pupils are immigrant, compared with only 15%

immigrants in the ordinary schools of the ILEA. The 1970 figures are even more alarming, for even though immigrants comprise nearly 17% of the normal school population, nearly 34% of the ESN school population is immigrant. And four out of five immigrant children in these ESN schools are West Indians.

"The same ILEA report gives figures of immigrant children whom the headmasters of these ESN schools thought were wrongly assessed and placed".

Bernard continued: "Three of the nineteen schools thought that less than 10% of their immigrant pupils had been wrongly placed; three thought that between 10 and 19 per cent were wrongly placed; a further three thought that the figure was between 20% and 29%. One school put the figure at between 30% and 39%; two schools thought that as many as 40% to 49% of the immigrant pupils were wrongly placed; and, finally, one school estimated that between 70% and 79% of its immigrant pupils were wrongly placed!"

Black children could not identify themselves with the school curricula, on which teachings were essentially eurocentric, which ignored the cultures and positive differences of Black pupils.

The British education system at the time created a sense of insecurity in the minds of Black pupils. Black pupils were taught that Eurocentric values were the source of world civilisation and 'black' was negative and non-productive, 'white' represents respect, beauty, wisdom and strength.

White Britain's subliminal cultural messages to the Black immigrants, as demonstrated in the mass media - press, radio and television, when they came, were suggestions of Black inferiority, for example, the very English language talked about: "as black as sin", "as black as a spade", "black leg", "black day", "black list", "black mail", "black market", "black sheep of the family", etc.

That social environment created low self-esteem. Black teenagers experienced a type of pervading social pressure. Many were homeless, unable to obtain apprenticeships and substantive training to gain skills to improve their quality of life. There was strong indication of deprivation, depression and dissatisfaction.

What British Society freely allowed immigrant children were social instability, menial and dead-end jobs, sex and more sex, dancing and sports. In short, unskilled jobs, free love, and regular visits to shebeen (underground basement parties - forerunner of 'raves') and youth clubs.

Britain did not offer proper culturally sensitive education, housing at reasonable mortgage and rent, skills and representations in the general administration of society.

The Black Community fought back and gave birth to the Black Supplementary Education Movement in 1970.

The momentum began in March 1969 when the London Borough of Haringey Council on the recommendation of its Education Committee, agreed to implement a dispersing of the Borough's immigrant children among the Borough's eleven comprehensive schools. Subsequently, the London Borough of Ealing adopted this type of policy. The process of dispersing the children was called 'banding'.

Haringey Borough Council's Education Committee Report of March stated: *"That for educational and social reasons and in the best long-term interests of the community as a whole, we must take steps to integrate the immigrant population by sharing it throughout all our schools on the basis of academic ability"*

A confidential report by the Vice-Chairman of the Education Committee, Alderman A.J.F. Doulton, who was also the headmaster of the public Highgate School, suggested the motive for the new 'banding' policy of the Council. The report stated: "*On a rough calculation about half of the immigrants will be West Indians at seven of the eleven schools, the significance of this being, the general recognition that their IQ's work out below their English contemporaries. Thus academic standards will be lower in schools where they form a large group.*"

The report also called attention to the increasing tendency of immigrant pupils to stay on beyond the school-leaving age and the consequent growth of non-academic sixth-forms. "*It is a process that will continue and it could particularly affect Haringey where the immigrant parents will see education as a way to open doors for their children*"

Three days after the official report was released, North London West Indian Association (NLWIA) organised the first protest demonstration outside Haringey Borough's Civic Centre.

Pamphlets[5] were printed and distributed, open meetings for parents were held, parents committee formed, a televised national press conference was called, and a protest petition containing the signatures of 928 local West Indian parents was handed in to the Council. An alliance was also made with the White middle class residents in the Borough who opposed the banding scheme for their own reasons.

The solidarity between Black And White parents gave NLWIA access to confidential reports and media contacts. The Conservative Party controlled Haringey Borough Council at the time. The banding programme was implemented for a short time, until the Labour Party took control of the Council in May 1971. The policy of dispersing children was stopped by the incoming Labour Administration.

The publicity and participation in the protest against banding, created awareness in the minds of Black parents and the Black Community in general. They recognised the hostility within the education system against Black children. Parents were able to understand in a more meaningful way, the implications of Black children being placed into Educational Sub-normal Schools.

Members of the Black Community took their struggles a step further and formed the Caribbean Educationists Association, later to be called the Caribbean Education And Community Workers Association (CECWA) during the summer of 1970 and called a three day seminar in August, 1970. The purpose of the seminar was:

- *"To improve our [members of the Black Community] background knowledge of the Caribbean society from which many of the children have come and with whose consciousness we are linked; and*

- *To focus on the changing relationships and problem which the black child experiences in British society."*

Black parents' awareness of the British school system continued to increase. That was an important landmark because Black parents believed that teachers in British schools were like those they knew in the Caribbean. However, Black teachers in British schools confirmed in public meetings that racism was rampant in many of the schools which Black children were attending in the 1960s and 70s. On the strength of that new information,

Black parents called for members of the Black Community to have greater involvement in the education of their children.

In the light of that new awareness in the Black Community, CECWA took on the leadership to gain proper education for Black children in British schools, and set about in defining what was meant by 'proper education'. According to CECWA Manifesto, 'proper education' meant *"an education which adequately prepares the black child to take his rightful place in society as one of its citizens as well as one which helps him to realise his own identity and self-image."*

After a number of discussions, CECWA came up with the idea of Black Supplementary Schools. The Black parents form four supplementary schools: Albertina Sylvester, George Padmore, Kwame Nkrumah and George Washington Carver. Subsequently, CECWA gave way to the Caribbean Teachers Association (CTA), one of the guiding lights was Trevor Carter, born in Trinidad. CTA was made up of professional teachers

Supplementary schools taught numeracy, literacy, history of the African and Caribbean people. Some taught drama. The Black Supplementary Movement spread across the country rapidly and supported by West Indian immigrants settlements during the early 1970s.

Supplementary schools were organised by nearly all the Black Power groups and they held conferences to exchange experiences, and discuss objectives. In Leeds, during 1971, after the publication of Bernard Coard's book, the West Indian Afro Brotherhood organised a conference with the United Caribbean Association, on Black children in ESN schools. The Conference agreed to set up a Supplementary School to assist the local children in need. CECWA convened its national

44

conference on supplementary schools on 23rd January, 1972. Supplementary schools became a way of life for many members of the Black Community as they experienced racism in the British school system. Both the Black middle class and the working class sent their children to Black Supplementary Schools, which were usually held on Saturday mornings. A school with a large pupil/student attendance, lessons might be extended to Saturday afternoons.

Teachers were normally qualified and parents paid a fee for their children's tuition, which might last for three to four hours weekly. The age group of attendance started from five to eighteen years of age. The older students might need extra tuition to pass the general certificate of education (GCE) examinations.

The Black Supplementary Education Movement gained popularity because parents saw improved academic performances in their children's work after attending supplementary schools. Many of those who improved were those whom state school failed to motivate, and likely to pass by. Other Black pupils attended Saturday schools to maintain their high academic standards.

The creation of the Black Supplementary School Movement demonstrated the historical resilience of members of the African People, in the face of serious social repression in Britain. The Black Supplementary Education Movement was another classic example of Black self-help.

In 1975, Len Garrison, born in Jamaica, set up The Afro-Caribbean Education Resource Project (ACER) in South West London, whose object was ' the provision of support for children of African heritage and those of other disadvantaged cultures, to enable them to achieve excellence in education'. ACER targeted teachers working in mainstream school provisions and provided and recommended teaching materials suitable for children of African heritage.

ACER, an independent initiative of the Black Community, was able to demonstrate[1] that pupils of middle years of schooling could be given a more equitable start in the classroom - that learning materials did not have to be only about one point of reference. Learning could take place from and about each other while children were allowed to share their own experiences. Children also showed that they respected each other more when the teachers and the classroom materials supported each other's point of view. ACER's learning materials had shown that they could provide an important lead in this work.

Twenty years later, the Black Supplementary Movement has become a model for trustees and governors of private fee paying, grant maintained and state schools, at their attempts to be placed high up on the government school league tables, in order to attract more pupils for their prestige and economic viability. Racism has become more pronounced, however, in these circumstances as children are excluded from schools, the highest proportion of whom are those of African origins.

---

[1] Len Garrison, Director, ACER Centre, ' Resources For Education In a Plural Society: 'Policy To Practice', Published in Self-Help News, Issue No 6. Published by The National Federation of Self-Help Organisations, 1986, London.

7. Black Youth And Social Pressures 1960-1975

Over 60% of Black youth left school yearly at the age of sixteen. The Dennis Stevenson's year-long independent survey published in July 1970, showed that although the unemployment figures for the Black population were below the national average, Black youth in the 16-24 age group had a startling proportion of 22% out of work - four times that of White youth. One found the unemployed Black youth passing their time at amusement centres, coffee bars and on the streets.

That was the social foundation Britain was building for the future. That was the 1970s. One should have been able to imagine the accumulative social, economic and political effects of this type of social inequality would have on the wider society in twenty years time, during the 1990s.

Black youth experiences set the stage for petty crimes and anti-social behaviours which were to last for decades.   Society protected itself by sentencing more and more Black youth of our inner cities, to custodian punishments for petty and street crimes. Social security 'safety net' did not help much, because those youth fell through that net. One Assistant Governor of a borstal remarked at the time that the number of Black boys being sent to borstals was 'causing some concern'.

It seemed inhumane for a society to put its citizens into low grade schools and later when they reached working age, failed to employ them, thus forcing the young unemployed into petty crimes.

Leslie, 17, born in Jamaica, arrived in England on his sixth birthday to join his parents. Leslie lived in North

47

London, and was educated at the local secondary modern. Leslie left school at sixteen, without the usual general certificate of education. Having left school, he found it difficult to get a job in 1972

Leslie said: "I read in the local press about a vacancy for trainee machine operator. I went to the firm that morning for an interview. When I got there, they said the vacancy was filled, which I did not believe. I left the office and phoned back ten minutes later and enquired about the same job, but this time I put on a cockney accent. They told me that the post was vacant and I should come for an interview. I didn't go. I phoned them to make sure that I was rejected because of my colour.

"I ended up taking a job as a messenger. At least I am moving about outside. I know that there is no future in this job," concluded Leslie.

On the other hand, David, 17, Black, born in England of Nigerian parentage, tried to get himself a suitable job as a trainee electrician after leaving school. He signed on at the local youth Employment Office (YEO).

The local YEO failed to place David. During his first two months of unemployment, he got Department of Social Security assistance of £6.50p per week, out of which he paid £4 for weekly rent. The remainder was for food and other expenses. After two months unemployment, his social security benefits were withdrawn.

David continued: "The Social Security people said that they were not going to give me any more money. I asked them how they expected me to live. They said I should find a job. After a week, my landlord threatened to throw me out of my bed-sit.

"That was when I decided to nick things. I started to steal money when I could and paid my rent, bought food and clothes. I also began to shop-lift things. At first it was difficult for me to do; but I got used to it. I got caught and the courts put me on two years probation.

"I was lucky. Some of my friends who couldn't find work and started stealing to survive got caught and sent to borstals, detention centres and prisons. Some of them, when they come out, find it more hard to get jobs, and so they have to start stealing again. Next thing you know, they're inside again!" David concluded.

Meanwhile, the number of unemployed youth turning to petty crime was on the increase - in particular in the big cities.

Those who managed to get employment of their choice had another type of complaint, their promotion prospects were blighted by prejudices and racism.

Lawrence, a 22 year old bank clerk, who lived in North London, was educated in England, and gained five 'O' levels and four 'A' levels in the General Certificate of Education (GCE) he complained that his promotion chances at the bank were very slim.

Lawrence told a story of how he joined Barclays Bank, DCO, in their Central Clearing Office, in London in 1968, with several White colleagues with less qualifications, and to his surprise, his White colleagues were placed 'on the scale' - on jobs which were known in the bank to bring promotion.

Lawrence: "New Black recruits to the bank are encouraged to take their banking examinations, which they invariably do. But when the Black recruits are qualified, they are not promoted, except for those who are returning permanently to their countries of origin, where they are expected to work for Barclays".

Lawrence gave an example of a friend, another Black, 'behind the scenes' bank clerk who had been working in the same bank for seven years, had a BSc degree in Economics and an Associate of the Institute of Banking, but there was no sign of his being promoted, though he had to train White recruits and later watched them climb to promotional heights. Lawrence and his friend planned to leave the bank.

Black youth had an air of resentment against those who limited their opportunities and stagnate their growth, in order that the youth could not employ their abilities to the full. Subsequently, that type of resentment led to dangerous social unrest in Britain's inner cities - a baptism of fire, which saw many inner cities set a light. Scenes which were only witnessed during the blitz of World War II, costing the government, local authorities and the insurance companies, millions of pounds.

As a result of such massive social rejection of Black people by White Britain, in the key areas of housing, education and employment, Black people could not reasonably integrate or assimilate in Britain's wider institutions, and so Black people developed their own social, economic and community political organisations, based on current pressing needs, with help from some members of White Britain.

In addition, Black children who were born and or brought up in Britain, were not prepared to be passive and take menial jobs as their parents did. Members of the new generation were articulate and militant in their demands for social justice.

C.L.R. James the Trinidadian writer and philosopher said at the Metro Youth Club, Ladbroke Grove, in West London on 4 January, 1971, on the occasion of his seventieth birthday:

"There is something new here in the young men and young women. I have seen them, and I have made enquiries, that there is a present generation that has grown up in Britain.

"They have been to school with the British children, have had the same lessons, have eaten the same food. They are now as ready to eat 'egg and chips' as to eat curry. That's what they've eaten in school here, and that's how they've grown up.

"Their parents are ready to accept discrimination. They came here and took jobs on the buses, they came here and took jobs washing dishes, they came here and took jobs on the railways.

"Their present generation says 'NO'. We will have the same kind of jobs as everybody else otherwise we are going to fight to the end.' That's why I'm glad to be here.

" May I end by saying that your future is the future of Great Britain; and the future of Great Britain is your future. If you make it, then it means that Britain will be making it, and if you don't make it, then the Britain there is will not be making it, and there will have to be a new Britain. Not only for you, but for all the oppressed everywhere."

8.   Cruel Social Conditions Created   Urban Street Soldiers

Black youth were victims of a cruel social environment during the 1970s. A section of British White media would have us believe that Black young people were thieves, who knocked old White people over their heads and took away their shopping and house keeping money - muggers !

That young Blacks did not want to work, and they lived off the State. They were noisy and undisciplined, went about in gangs, and the little intelligence they have, they kept for primitive music and sex.

Here you have character assassinations on a massive scale. That situation was worsened by some police divisions in areas of high density of Black settlers. Un-tested police statistics of alleged 'black crimes' were released to the Press.   The Police were playing the 'number game' - an attempt to shock citizens into taking reactionary decisions, and starting a 'White Backlash' against Black people in Britain.

A large number of the figures released by the police about 'Black Crimes' were based on Black young people who had been picked up by the police and charged with "being a suspected person, loitering with intent to commit an arrestable offence, contrary to section 4 of the Vagrancy Act 1824."

The majority of the youngsters protested their innocence; but, because of the difficulty of proving innocence on such a charge for which the police need not produce physical evidence to back up their allegations, over 99% of those so charged were convicted by the magistrates courts. Unfortunately, the person so charged cannot choose to be tried by judge and jury.

On conviction, what followed was something resembled a 'witch hunt' of young Black citizens.

Perhaps Black people should never have responded to Britain's plea for help, in the 1950s, during the period of her intense labour shortage. Nevertheless, Black people came, and Britain got on her feet again.

On the face of it, White Britain was ungrateful. However, whatever the difficulties, Black mums and dads stuck it out so that their children might have a better chance to make good in society.

Black people lived in very poor housing conditions and paid high rents to exploiting private landlords. Peter Rachman,[6] Polish born of Jewish parents and Landlord Extraordinary, provided flats for members of the West Indian Community at six times the market rate. Few landlords were prepare to let flats to Black people, particularly in Notting Hill, West London during the 1950s and early 1960s. Referring to Rachman and his relationship with the West Indian immigrant community at the time, a West Indian social worker summed it up: "He'd ask £6 a week for a flat that a controlled tenant would have paid £1 for". This type of exploitation came to be known as "Rachmanism". Peter Rachman was not the only landlord who exploited Black tenants, only the others had not achieve the notoriety as he did. It was particularly ironic when Rachman himself experienced serious hardships, being an ex-Nazi concentration camp detainee.

Mortgages and council flats were difficult to get. There were additions to the family, and children left behind soon joined their parents. Those who were too young to go to school should have gone to nursery and playcentres, but Black parents found it difficult to get their children into nurseries and play centres.

Many turned to illegal child minders, and some parents could not even pay for that service, and so some children were left at home on their own. This sometimes resulted in mental cruelty and, in a number of cases, Black children died in paraffin heater fires and other home accidents.

Because of low wages[7] and their proud objection to State help, some Black parents go out to work for long hours, to support their children.

Having suffered serious mental cruelty and exposed to injurious environmental conditions in his/her infancy, the Black child started schooling. Many parents had no idea about the workings of the British school system. They sent their children to any school - the more convenient, the better. In the evenings, some children waited at friends' houses after school. Sometimes the unlucky ones played on the streets and in the parks.

The schools which many Black children attended were normally over-crowded with a high turn over of teachers. Because of the social problems at home - overcrowding and lack of parental appreciation of the School System, the average Black child was unable to get the sort of home support required to benefit from the positive side of the school. As the children grew older, they began to show the results of their sufferings and lack of adequate attention during their early years.

The first people to see the Black child's reaction, protest, anger, etc. were the teachers, who were generally White and who were least likely to understand the real reason for the child's behaviour. The child was invariably given intelligence tests and later placed in 'special' schools - remedial, educational sub-normal, etc. - which further restricted his/her development. Then truancy sets in. To the child, the School programme became irrelevant, and that was the beginning of the Black child's fight against the System.

Next to come into contact with the child were his hardworking parents (or parent, if the child was being brought up in a single parent family) who were being exploited by their employers; but they continued to accept their exploitation and insults because they wanted to give their children a better life.

Parents learned that their child was not attending school regularly or that the education authority had placed their child in a 'special school'. Some parents were unable to communicate with their child. There were quarrels because child and parents were confused or disillusioned. The parents had not been able to attend parents/teachers meetings. They had been too tired after a hard day's work, or they felt that they would not be made to feel welcome at parents/teachers meetings.

The child continued to argue with parents, and the family Television set became the child's primary educator. The TV taught love and hate; war and peace; honesty and dishonesty, among other values; but what was clear to the Black child was that his/her Race was hardly represented in a positive way on the TV, and so TV had not helped the Black child to answer his/her innermost questions: 'Who Am I ?; What Am I ? and Where Am I Going ?'

As the Black child reaches adolescence his/her problems grew up with him/her. The school did not understand him/her. His/her parents - busy winning the bread for the family, had not found time to understand him/her; and his/her friends, who understood him/her could not do anything about the problem because they, too, had similar problems.

The child, along with his Black contemporaries, took to the streets, building up a sub-culture. One which rejected mainstream British culture and set about trying to appreciate their parents' culture; but not wanting to be totally submissive to that culture.

It was a sub-culture which demanded respect for the person. One which rejected British hypocrisy and orthodox moral standards and values, and one which was daring and creative, with a strong sense of survival, by any means that was necessary.

The average Black child, because of his/her deprived background, had not achieved academic excellence at school, not because he/she was incapable of learning, but because he/she was not motivated by his/her parents, teachers and social environment to achieve 'excellence' within a White-dominated System. The Black male was particularly vulnerable.

Yet there were those, 'above average Black children', whose parents, teachers and their immediate social environment motivated them to achieve brilliance in their school work. Subsequently, some of these achievers got disillusioned with Society which failed to reward them with suitable jobs, responsibility and financial remuneration.

As a whole, the Black child had not been given adequate careers guidance at, and on leaving, school.

The Black child's protests and bitterness increased, and he/she soon found that he/she was in conflict with the police and the courts. The child began to learn about social workers, child care officers, probation officers, psychiatrists and educational psychologists. He/she got put into local authority's care, placed into community homes, given or denied bail and legal aid. He got sent to remand homes, remand centre, detention centre, borstals and prisons.

Later, he/she got sent to mental institution, where he/she was given excess tranquillisers and sedatives, which often resulted in dramatic personality changes. (This was the very early stages of the authorities 'experimenting' on members of the Black Community, using chemicals as a means of social control, which was to become a major issue twenty years later.)

The Black child who remained at home, until his/her adolescence, found, at age sixteen, he/she could not cope with his/her authoritarian parents and left home impulsively. Young men readily took this option. Not knowing where to go, and having nowhere to sleep, and often without a job, and no money in their pockets. They 'jumped from frying pan into the fire', as it were. They got very little sympathy or encouragement from Society. The new homeless Black youth ended up sleeping on friends' floors, or got arrested for being a 'suspected person' and sent to a remand home. Some slept at bus termini, railway and tube stations, or in derelict houses and parks (during the summer).[8]

Homeless Black youth learnt about legal squats and they took advantage of the law. That helped to reduce dramatically the levels of some homelessness among Black youth on the street. The Black Community began to develop short stay hostel projects for homeless youth, like the Dashiki Council and The Harambee Projects (These pioneering Black Community initiatives will be discussed elsewhere in this book).

Squatting was not a permanent solution, since a normal squat lasted for an average of six months before a court order was obtained, by the local authority or private owners, after which the young squatters looked elsewhere for another house. This presented a continuos state of insecurity to the squatters, at a time when the Law Commission's presented its final report to the Home Office on conspiracy and trespass, whose recommendations formed the basis of the Government Bill to make squatting in certain instances a criminal offence.

Meanwhile, however, the Black youngsters continued to experience problems, especially in getting jobs, apprenticeships and other training in skilled trade. Surveys done over a ten year period showed that Black youngsters' rate of unemployment rose far above the national average.

The National Census of 1971 showed that 16.2% Black youth were without jobs. Five years later, the Political And Economic Planning Survey showed, that the situation had deteriorated. The young people looked for jobs, but many were unable to get them, in view of the current economic climate and basic prejudices of White Society against people of colour. Not many gained lasting benefits under the government job creation programmes which were introduced, during the 1970s, which also targeted the long term unemployed.

Equally, a significant number of Black young people refused to return to the Social Security for financial assistance, because they had been to the careers office, employment office and the social security office and failed to get financial assistance in times of needs.

Many young people did not always understand the bureaucratic processes through which they were expected to pass before they received money. Many walked out of the offices never to return.

Others waited and found that what was being offered to live on was an insult to their persons - not enough to cover their expenses. That situation put the young people at greater risks.

It was from that experience the attitude developed that 'we won't starve', which led to petty crimes, stealing money to survive, as they saw it, in a monetary society, in which everything had to be paid for.

That was therefore the beginning of a career in penal institutions by many Black youngsters. As a result, because some street crimes were known to have been committed by Black youngsters - a small minority, Black young people continued to be picked up by the police and placed on 'Sus'.[9] That situation increased tension between the police and Black youth.

Non-employment of Black youth led to Black recidivism, particularly of those who came from a poor and working class background.

Ironically, a number of the unemployed young people, who were picked up by the police, charged, taken to court, convicted and fined, found it necessary to go out and commit more petty street crimes in order to pay the court fines. These young people's anti-social behaviour sprang from their first and fundamental instinct for survival.

Every street crime, which was committed by the youngsters, was deemed to have been committed by Society. The young people were puppets on a string of social circumstances, which was being manipulated by Society - the Legislators, Executives, Judiciary, the Administrators and the Church. All had a part in this. If not, what effective action did they take to bring a sense of identity, self-esteem and purpose to these youngsters.

When a youngster taken to court and placed in the dock, Society should also be placed on trial. But there was not a court big enough to hold Society, and then, who would have been the Judge and jury - perhaps the victims of social controls should fill those places.

Young Black people - like a number of White working class young people, were scapegoats to a failed British Social Order, and so, Society built a cage around poor Black and White youths, which crippled the mind, creating a bandage of illiteracy and ignorance, dampened the spirit and bruised the soul. A cage that caused working class youngsters to flow in and out of penal institutions, until they seemed totally 'institutionalised', as chronic recidivism set in.

To many of our Black people living in Britain and elsewhere, because of social injustices, from their conception until death, their lives would have been a misery, partly because they were born Black and poor, living in a predominantly White and capitalist structure,

When one dared to look in the faces of some of our young Black people, from whom hope was removed by indifference and racism, one saw **pain.** They were being socially 'killed' daily by British 'tolerance' and 'fair play'. Black youth were being pressured into a dome of degradation. They were being crushed by British 'affluence'. Black youth lashed out, any which way they could.

Their cries came from the remedial, educationally sub-normal, low grade and 'approved' schools, the remand and detention centres, borstals and prisons, and the psychiatric establishments . They cried out from the police stations and courts. They cried out during their lonely hours, walking the streets, searching for accommodation and jobs. To many, they had given up searching, because they had searched enough and found nothing, and every refusal was salt in an already open and bleeding psychological wound.

Black youth cried out and say - *'Babylon, let me be free; let me discover myself; let me breath; let me be !'*

But it seemed that those cries floated away on the winds of British indifference.

The attitude of young people was that Society must listen to their plight. Black leadership at the time believed that young people must force Society to listen. That young people must move forcefully forward towards their destiny, with the **Sword** for Justice and the **Key** for Opportunity, and that there could be no compromise, short of total and complete human respect and integrity. The sort of demands which their peers were putting forward in apartheid South African Black townships, albeit in a more dramatic and physical manner, the price of which a number of Black young people paid with their lives. 'That could never happen in Britain', was the talk at the time, until the fires came to Britain's inner cities a decade later.

By the late 1970s, Britain's accumulated social and economic injustices had created fearless urban street fighters, particularly among young people of African origins, British citizens.

Therefore, the British Establishment to avoid a significant confrontation between working class Black youth supported by their White friends, the machinery of social injustices had to have been removed. It was not.

The seeds of injustices in education, housing, employment and the criminal justice system at the lower courts, were allowed to flourish, on the wings of racist bigotry, and so Britain should reasonably expect to reap some of the fruits of her labour, however, long she had to wait. Equally, if Britain had sewed the seeds of social justice, she should be expected to reap the fruits of her endeavours, however long she had to wait.

The choice was made, and because that conflicted with the pure principles of natural justice, we set ourselves up to reap the fruits of conflict in the ensuing years. The CONFRONTATION had arrived.

9. Black Pressure Groups And Their Response To Social Repression In Britain 1945- 1975

By 1969 the social and economic conditions of Black people in Britain were of such that the immigrants began to develop pressure groups to protect their interests within a democracy. The 1960s and 70s saw a period of massive change, not only in Britain but across the world.

It was during that period Mr Harold Macmillan, British Conservative Prime Minister, said that the British people 'never had it so good'. When he went to African, he told the White settlers that 'the winds of change were blowing through Africa - perhaps a warning of things to come.

Africans were suing for independence. The 'die' of destiny had been cast by the 5th Pan African Congress organised by Amy Ashwood Garvey, the late Marcus Mosiah Garvey's wife in Manchester in 1945. A new Pan-African Order was heralded.

The Conference[10] resolved that the people of the British colonies must free themselves from the yoke of colonialism. At that meeting were some of Black history's prominent figures - Kwame Nkrumah, Jomo Kenyatta, George Padmore and others. By the late 1950s and early 1960s those attended the Manchester Conference were agitating in Africa and the Caribbean for independence of their countries from British colonial rule. Their agitation were based, to a significant extent, on Marcus Garvey's philosophy of 'Africa for the Africans at home and abroad'; 'African self determination' and 'Building of African Nationhood'.

Kwame Nkrumah took the boldest steps of all, being one of the prime movers of the Organisation of African Unity (OAU), which had its Inaugural Summit at Addis Ababa, May 1963.

The British race relations situation must also be seen in the context of current international events. The USA was engaged in a war in Vietnam, South East Asia, and the cream of her sons refused to go and fight in Vietnam, and so many draft dodgers came to Europe, and joined the 'Flower Power People', popular alternative culture at the time, whose participants advocated 'make love - not war'. They were generally referred to as the 'hippies'.

Jamaicans gained independence in 1962. The majority of immigrants from the Caribbean during the 1950s and 60s were Jamaicans. Jamaica along with Trinidad, Guyana, Ghana, Kenya and Nigeria subsequently gained independence. By 1968, Nigeria was in a civil war. The Eastern Region, called Biafra, broke away from the Federal State of Nigeria.

Elsewhere in Africa, Mr Macmillan's 'winds of change' were erupting into gale force, as Africans took up arms against their colonial powers, commencing in the 1950s throughout the 1960s.

Ghana, in 1950, pushed the process of African liberation forward as the Convention People's Party (CPP) led the Ghanaian people in 'Positive Action' campaign against British colonialism.

Kenya in 1952 saw the Land And Freedom Army (Mau Mau) launched armed struggle against British colonialism. Algeria War of independence started 1954, led by the Front de Liberation Nationale(FLN).

Guinea rejected 'assimilation with France and choose full independence in 1958. South Africa's armed struggle started in earnest, led by the Pan African Congress (PAC), founded by Mangaliso Sobukwe and other militant youth members of the African National Congress in 1959, which was intensified in 1960, in the light of the massacre of unarmed Africans at Sharpeville and Langa.

The Congo armed struggle got going in 1960, led by the Movement Feminine de la Solidarity Africa (MFSA) organised by Andree Bloum. Angola, revolutionary war of independence got on the way in 1961, after Portuguese ignore a petition from the Popular Movement for the Liberation of Angola (MPLA), appealing for peaceful political reform.

In 1963, Guinea Bissau's time came for a war of liberation in 1963, which was guided by the African Independence Party of Guinea and Cape Verde (PAIGC), led by Amilcar Cabral, against the Portuguese. Namibia in 1966 saw the start of armed struggle for independence led by South West Africa People's Organisation (SWAPO).

Zimbabwe (Rhodesia) on 28th April, 1966 saw the second Chimurenga (war of liberation) led by the Zimbabwe African National Union (ZANU). Mozambique of 1964 entered its military phase of the revolution under the guidance of the Front for the Liberation of Mozambique (FRELIMO) led by Eduardo Chivambo Mondlane.[11]

The American civil rights activities took a dramatic turn in 1955 in Montgomery, when Rosa Parks refused to give up her seat on the bus, which precipitated a year long boycott by the African-American people, which was organised by the National Association for the Advancement of Coloured People (NAACP). The Black Civil Rights Movement subsequently recruited Reverend Dr. Martin Luther King Jr, Leader of the Southern Baptist

Conference, whose civil rights message touched the soul of the World.

What seemed to have been upper most in the minds of Black immigrants in Britain was the common link of their demands for civil rights and that which was going on in the USA civil rights movement and the African Liberation struggles, including the anti-apartheid activities in South Africa, with high profile personalities like Nelson and Winnie Mandela, wife and husband team. Black people, mindful of their common experiences, concluded that there was a common enemy.

The Global African Community recognised and began to practise 'unity in diversity', which said that Black People must work in unity, with themselves and others who share their aspirations for natural justice. Victims and potential victims of racism, xenophobia and religious intolerance must ensure that they did not internalised their conditions. They recognised that Black People were not the enemy of freedom, equality and justice. History pointed to whom and what that enemy was.

In the USA, some of the descendants of Africans, who were made slaves by Caucasians, were moving away from Christianity, the former slave owners' Religion, to The Nation Of Islam, founded by Wallace D. Fard , a Caucasian , in 1930, and now led by Elijah Muhammad , an African, and offspring of those who were made slave by the descendants of the people who now enforced racism and injustices, in the 1960s. Elijah Muhammad, was a follower of The Honourable Marcus Mosiah Garvey, 1887-1940, the Father of Pan-Africanism. The Honourable Elijah Muhammad's message was "dedicated to the resurrection of the Black man and woman of America and the World".

The White media called the Nation of Islam "Black Muslim". Malcolm X , El Hadji Malik El Shabazz (Malcolm Little), an African-American, came on the scene as a brave champion for Black people in the USA, during the 1960s. Black people in Britain, because of their experiences, could and did relate to Malcolm's speeches on race and politics.

At the same time, The Black Panther Movement, whose membership was made up of poor Black people living in the American ghettos, was challenging USA Police repression. Reverend Martin Luther King, Jr. - now Leader of the Southern Baptist Conference, a non-violent Christian organisation of churches - was saying the same thing about civil rights. Stokely Carmichael,(now called Kwame Ture), Leader of the Non-violent Student Organisation (SNCC), was also challenging racism.

The Rastafarian Movement, emanated from Jamaica, emphasised 'culture and redemption'. Rasta message was in their music and appearances. That Movement had profound impact on the Black youth of Britain during the 1960s and 70s, particularly those from the Caribbean. Yet the Rasta did not follow leaders, except their belief in the divinity of His Imperial Majesty Haile Selassie. Bob Marley, Peter Tosh, Marcia Griffith, naming but a few, all born in Jamaica, brought in their music, a synthesis of the Spirit of Black People - the African People.

The core demands of all these world activists were anti-racism, freedom, equlity and justice. This created high awareness in the minds of Black people in Britain. What they read in the press, heard on the radio and saw on TV, confirmed that their stance against injustice in Britain was the right one. Moreover, they were only a very small part of a world movement for civil and human rights.

British Black people, therefore, reinforced their civil rights organisations and intensified their popular demands for fair play for all in society, and they suffered very badly in that struggle. British prisons were being populated by young Black people as a direct result of Black youth standing up for their civil rights.

The call for justice threw up a number of Black pressure groups in Britian's inner cities at the time. The Universal Coloured People Association (UCPA) was one of the first West Indian organisations operated in England, which was based in London. Two leading lights were Michael Bartlett and Rene Webb, both born in Jamaica and George Joseph, born in Trinidad, Webb was a British ex-serviceman who served in World War II.

The West Indian Standing Conference (WISC) was set up in 1959, in response to the killing of West Indian Kelsor Cochrane, a carpenter, in 1959, at the hands of White racist thugs, 'Teddy boys', in Notting Hill Gate, West London. WISC, whose leading light was Jeff Crowford, was at the peak of its effectiveness. It brought to members of the wider public the racist and, at times, murderous nature of some British citizens, in their response to Black people, who came to support Britain in her hour of need. Some of the other leading lights were: Glem Byfield, born in Jamaica, Joe Hunte, born in St. Kits and Nevis, Cliff Lynch, Len Dyke, Alan Kelly, and Glenda Forde all born in Jamaica, William Trant, born in Monsterrat and Ralf Straker, born in Barbados.

The Membership of WISC was made up of those first generation of West Indians to Britain in the early 1950s and 60s. The ones who were described as 'model citizens' by British establishment figures and government ministers. The Police and the British courts hardly had any occasion to come in serious contact with this older generation of West Indians. The immigrant took that which were offered and got on with the business of saving to return 'back home'. Many remarked at the time "this is ice box country. Not home for me". Given the Immigrant attitude of this nature, the *status quo* of White Britain, racism and all, was left unchallenged. This position began to change when members of the 'Coloured' Community felt the pinch of racism, as they experienced assault, battery and murder, at the hands of racists.

At the time, a significant area of land mass in the Caribbean and African were still under British colonial rule. The last real challenge to this colonial strength was made by Jamaican born Marcus Mosiah Garvey, 1884 - 1940, and his Universal Negro Improvement Association and African Communities League founded in 1914, which later recorded an international membership of six million, when Marcus Garvey was only 33 years old. That success was based essentially on his basic philosophy of Black self-help, self-esteem and self determination.

By the late 1960s, Black young people who entered Britain as children of first generation immigrant, and those born in Britain, took a fundamentally different stance from that of their parents. They refused to accept the British *status quo*, which was soiled by Racism. Black youth understood and identified with Marcus Garvey basic philosophy of self-esteem, self-help and personal self-determination.

WISC had done and continued to do important work in the West Indian Community. It was, however, time for a change. The current pressing social circumstances demanded a change. The Black Community needed a generalist organisation, with which a multi-cultural community under pressure could identify, particularly second and third generation of Black young people. The West Indian Standing Conference lost its young membership to more challenging pressure groups.

THE CAMPAIGN AGAINST RACIAL DISCRIMINATION (CARD), one of Britain's first multi-racial race relations initiatives (1957-70), based in Brent, North London, served the community well, exposing the racial prejudices in society. One of the leading lights of CARD was the late Dr David Pitt, born in Grenada, West Indies. He was a British Labour Party Member.

The Rt. Honourable Enoch Powell, then Conservative member of Parliament, predicted, in a speech he gave in Warsall, Birmingham, on February, 1968, which was later published in his book, *"Freedom And Reality"*,[12] that "As I look ahead I am filled with foreboding. Like the Roman, I seem to see 'The River Tiber foaming with much blood'... Only resolute and urgent action will avert it now"

Powell's speech was well received by the White working class Dockers and Porters in Smithfield, London, who marched to the House of Commons in support of Enoch Powell.

Mr Powell wanted to stop Black people coming to Britain to settle, and his 'river of blood' speech contributed to a climate of suspicion, fear and hate, which ensured that Black citizens in Britain would never again feel safe or welcome in Europe.

That type of anti-Black speech also contributed to a spate of immigration laws in 1968, 1971 and 1981, which severely restricted people of black skin to immigrate to Britain from the New Commonwealth. The 1981 British Citizen Act gave a whole new meaning to

British Citizenship. After 1981, British Birth no longer guaranteed the individual British citizenship. This piece of legislation was framed with Black skin people in mind, which continued to echo Winston Churchill's Cabinet fears of 1954, when the foundation was laid to curtail equal rights to Black skin people in Britain.

The Indian Workers Association of Great Britain (IWA) 1959 represented the people from the subcontinent of India. *Race Collective* wrote, in its 'New Perspective On The Asian Struggle':[13] "The Indian Workers' Association had its origins in the social and cultural cohesiveness of the Punjabi community, way back in the late fifties and early sixties, when most of the immigrant to Southall and to Leicester and Derby and the industrial centres of the Midland was from the Jullunder and Hoshiatanis districts of Punjab.

"Starting as a cultural and social meeting place for immigrant workers, as a focus of nostalgia and national pride, the Indian Workers' Association rapidly become politicised as a consequence of the industrial struggles the members faced and, in the late sixties, in response to the immigration laws passed by the Labour government". The IWA had a Marxist foundation.

IWA worked with the British Black Panther Movement, The Black Unity And Freedom Party and other Black African-led groups in 1970s. When the Black Panther Movement took the initiative and called a National Conference On The Rights Of Black people, at the Alexandra Palace in North London, in 1971, the IWA sent 21 delegates by coach from Birmingham where the IWA was based.

Joint Indian and African/Caribbean solidarity was also demonstrated in 1968 and 1970 during a joint anti-immigration bill introduced by the Labour Government. Jim Callaghan was the Home Secretary at the time. The demonstration - the most massive - was also against "the Kenyan Asian Bill, passed by the Labour Government in record time (between conception as a Bill and execution as an Act, it went through the shortest gestation in British history).

Subsequently, the Asians from East Africa became vocal in the British Indian communities, particularly in areas as Leicester and Loughborough in the Midlands and Wilesden, North London, in industrial affairs and political matters. The Asians forged their own organisations like the Bangladeshi Welfare Association and the Bengali Housing Action Group (BHAG), in the East End of London. In Southall, the Southall Youth Movement and Southall Rights. In addition to those mentioned other primary Asian settlement concentrated in Birmingham, Bradford, Leamington Spa, Derby and Coventry.

The Asian communities, Indian and Pakistani, had their temples and mosques, whose religious leaders strongly influenced the social development of their local communities. Bangladeshi nationals living in Britain, on becoming a Nation, set up educational and welfare voluntary groups to provide culturally sensitive services to members. The Chinese had been established settlers in Central London and Manchester. Most were caterers, famous for their Chinese restaurants.

The family pattern of the average Asian at the time appeared traditional and solid. The Asian families did not have a history of slavery, as the Africans who came from the Caribbean. Crucially, the Asian had their mother tongue in tact. The people from the Caribbean did not. The English language was still 'on loan' by the former slave owners and colonial administrators.

The original languages and religions of the African people, who were forcefully transported to the Americas, including the Caribbean, were forbidden by Caucasian slave owners. Those Africans - most of whom came from West Africa, who insisted on speaking their ancestor's languages and practise their native religions, were seriously discouraged by the White plantation owners, to the extent of mutilations and lost of lives as examples to others.

Idi Amin, the President of Uganda, expelled the Asians from Uganda during the late 1960s, many of whom came to Britain. Many of these Asians seemed different from those who came direct from India and Pakistan. Many Ugandan Asian had money and assets in Britain. They could set up business without much difficulty, which many did.

The majority of Indians and Pakistani and later Bangladeshi came to Britain to improve their quality of life. Like the Africans from the Caribbean, the majority of Asians were economic immigrants and had very little or no capital or collateral to start business. Many worked in the factories alongside Africans from the Caribbean. The early 1970s witnessed strong Afro-Asian solidarity in Britain, specifically between those from India, Pakistan and later Bangladesh. Both the Pakistani and Bangladeshi communities continued to set up separate social, cultural and educational associations subsequently.

The Indian Workers' Association of Great Britain was, however, in the front line of the anti-racist struggles, for over two decades, marching and working with the people from the Caribbean. IWA (GB), with branches at various parts of England, including South England, London and Southall, Middlesex, was led by Jagmohan Joshi.

A certain type of prejudice seemed to have been introduced to the people of African descent in Britain by some of those Asians who came from East Africa. That could have been because of their expulsion from Africa.

East African Asians were invariably reminded by solidarity conscious people from the Caribbean and Africa that 'Africa was Africa and Britain was Britain'. It was an opportunity for all concerned to forge good friendship in Britain between all groups, which was necessary for community harmony, and that British type of racism did not need any additional support imported from abroad.

The Chinese had been consistently friendly and, on the face of it, maintained a neutral position. The Black immigrants had always had a friendly relationship with the British Chinese Community, particularly in Manchester and London. The majority of the British Chinese came from Hong Kong, a British colony at the time.

On 28 April, 1968, organisations from the Indian, Pakistani, African and Caribbean communities in Britain, called a joint meeting in Leamington Spa, in the Midlands. It was the first time that organisations catering for Africans, Caribbean and Asians peoples living in Britain decided to take united action in this way.

The Conference resolved to form itself into a BLACK PEOPLES ALLIANCE, 'A militant front for black consciousness and against racialism'. A National Steering Committee was formed and consisted of the following:[1]

1. Michael Bartlett, born in Jamaica, of the Universal Coloured Peoples Association (UCPA).
2. David Udo, born in Nigeria, West Africa, of the British Black Panther Movement (BPM).
3. Keith Miles, born in Jamaica, of the Youth Forces For Liberation (YFL).

---

[1] Minutes of Black Peoples' Alliance Inaugural Meeting 28 April, 1968

4. Zacharia Chowdhary, born in Pakistan, of the National Federation Of Pakistani Association (NFPA).
5. Ajmer Singh, born in India, Afro-Asian Association (AAA).
6. George Joseph, born in Trinidad, of the Universal Coloured People Association (UCPA).
7. A.S. Jouhl, born in India, of the Indian Workers Association (IWA).
8. T. Haq, born in Pakistan, of the National Federation of Pakistani Association (NFPA)
9. Allan Kelly, born in Jamaica, West Indian Standing Conference (WISC)
10. G. Archer, West Indian Progressive Union
11. Jagmohan Joshi, born in India, of the Indian Workers Association (IWA), who was also asked to act as Convenor of the Steering Committee of the Alliance.

The mailing address of the Alliance was at 1 Birch Croft, Birmingham 24. Produced below are minutes of the first meeting of the Alliance.

"DOCUMENTED AND ADOPTED AT THE INAUGURAL MEETING ON 28 APRIL, 1968

1. WHY HAS THE MEETING BEEN CALLED

This meeting has been called today because the oppressed black minorities are facing a *most serious situation*. The last couple of weeks events, with [Enoch] Powell's, [MP] speech and it's aftermath have highlighted this, but this was just one step in a continuous campaign which was started at the end of the 1950's by political parties to whip up racial antagonism and hatred to make political gains on the basis of racialism. We should be quite clear that in this respect there has been no distinction between the Conservative and Labour parties.

We need to examine racialism not just in isolation but as one aspect of the growth of Fascism in Britain and indeed the whole of Western Europe. As British capitalism has gone into ever deeper crises so we have seen the ruling class as represented now by the Labour Party, bringing Fascism into our midst. The attack on the working class standards of living and working class organisation, the growth of a corporate state cannot be looked upon in isolation from the growth of racialism.

Evidence from the Dockers marches and the political strikes in favour of racialism have indicated quite clearly that the political parties have now given the green light to the overtly fascist organisations and they are now very active in organising particularly amongst the working class. The situation is extremely serious and it is imperative that we take action immediately.

There are certain complexities in the present situation and this may account for the fact that not every one has seen clearly all the aspects of the situation in the past. It is a complex one for several reasons:
(A) Contradictions within the ruling class. The Labour party has often been regarded by the black minorities as the anti-racialist party. This underlines the cunningness of their

approach. For , while it is the Labour party who have introduced such measures as a weak Race Relations Act and now another bill as a sop to black and liberal opinion, they have also introduced some of the most vicious ant-immigrant, pro-racialist legislation. The Conservative have caused less confusion, because they have always taken a hard line, and even when [Edward] Health, [Prime Minister], removed [Enoch] Powell from the shadow Cabinet, he was careful to emphasise that he was not in any disagreement with *what* Powell said only the way he said it. If any confusion do still exist about the stand of the political parties we need to make it quite clear that neither is concerned with integration and both are equally prepared to use racialism as a political weapon.

(B) Just as there are certain contradictions within the ruling class, so the immigrants also have their differences. Within the immigrant community many middle class elements have often denied the existence of prejudice and discrimination or turned upon their community and blamed the working class section for being responsible for English hostility. Many of the middle class immigrants have been vehicles for government policies, e.g., immigrants representatives on the National Committee for Commonwealth Immigrants, and the British Government for their part tried to split the immigrant communities. Obviously the support of all section of the black communities should be sought but not at the cost of taking the soft line preferred by many of the middle class immigrants.

(C) Further contradictions appear between the national minorities. They have been suspicious of one another and have sometimes seen their interests as conflicting, e.g. over the Kenyan Asians. This meeting is one of the most concrete signs of us overcoming these differences.

(D) A further complicating factor is the role of the British working class. The black immigrants are the most oppressed section of the working class here but the indigenous working class is also oppressed. They have suffered severe attacks on their standard of living in recent years but for a number of reasons they have not always blamed the capitalist system and their representatives for either Labour or Conservatives for their ill fate, and have in fact taken on an anti-black immigrant stand. There are a number of reasons for this, including the whole background of imperialism which has resulted in the inculcation of racialist attitudes among the carried class; also there has been no political party which has carried out consistent campaigns exposing Government policy in attempting to use the black minorities as a scapegoat for their policies. The action of certain section of the white working class is completely condemnable and cannot be excused under any circumstances.

2. WHAT DO WE WANT:

(A) Unite the black people against Racialism and Imperialism

(B) Fight racialism vigorously from all quarters, Labour Government, Tories, employers, unions, police, press, radio, T.V., etc..

(C) Expose the Labour Government racialist policies over:
- Immigration - demand repeal of 1962 Act.
- The number game. Not going in for how many should be let in, quotas, etc.,
- Phoney protections through marginal law like present Race Relations Bill, conciliation committee, etc..

(D) Seek allies from majority community but also expose false allies such as the do-gooders who have been using black organisations to further their own vested interests, political ambitions, etc.

3. HOW CAN WE ACHIEVE OUR ENDS ?

(A) Through forming the right kind of organising machinery. This can either be an umbrella type body or a co-ordinating committee. In this case, The Black Alliance.

(B) Through organising at the grass-roots level. Too many immigrant organisations are national or semi-national but do not have strong bases in the very areas where fascists are most active.

(C) Through organising immigrant workers at the place of work, factories, hospitals and other public places where immigrants work. Trade union aspects.

(D) Through undertaking the kinds of activities which will mobilise our own people and not necessarily the kinds of things which the British find most acceptable.

(E) Through conducting our own publicity and forcing the 'respectable obedient' so-called immigrant spokesman who are continuously being interviewed etc..

(F) Through making preparations for protection and security. This is an urgent task with growing assaults on person and property with little or no police protection and plenty of police intimidation. The need for the formation of vigilante patrols.

(G) Through anticipating growing unemployment among our ranks and taking necessary steps to mobilise unemployed workers.

(H) Co-ordinate efforts with the struggle against imperialism in the countries of origin"

While there had been solidarity between the African, the Caribbean, Indian and Pakistani civil rights organisations, the Black (African) civil rights initiatives were in the front line, the cutting edge of anti-racist struggles in Britain. Much of the focus of this book, therefore, will inevitably be on the activities of those at the sharp end of civil rights and anti-racist activities during the period.

During the 1960s and 70s, when the term 'black' or 'coloured' were used, they referred to people of African descent. Subsequently, the term 'black' was used in a political context, by some people. This presents some confusion, therefore, when the term 'Black and Asian' were used simultaneously.

The Police did not attack members of the Asian community as was the case with those of the African/Caribbean community, during the 1960s, early and mid 1970s. Those attacks came in 1979, in Southall, Middlesex and elsewhere in England. Until then, the Asians focused their targets on gaining industrial rights in the factories in which they worked, like Mansfield Hosiery Mills in Loughborough in 1973 and the Imperial Type-writers strike in Leicester in 1974. Grunwick strike in Willesden came later in 1977.

The Conservative, Labour and Liberal Parties did not think that the 'black vote' was of sufficient interest for which to canvass. This belief stayed until the 1990s when all the main British political parties recognised the importance of the 'black vote' and began to compete vigorously for it.

The new piece of Race Relations legislation passed by Parliament was not effective, and ironically, the first victim of the 1965 and 1968 Race Relations Acts was Michael DeFretas, Trinidadian, and President of The Racial Adjustment Action Society (RASS), based in North London. Mr DeFretas, (also known as Michael Abdul Malik and Michael X), was sentenced to one year imprisonment for alleged inciting racial hatred in

Reading, Berkshire after an alleged speech he made to West Indian nurses.

Black people felt as if they were on their own fighting racism and State repression, as they saw it.

That situation created a strong sense of urgency among members of the Black Community, particularly the young, who were a mixture of students, workers and the unemployed. Community and pressures groups were formed and consolidated, which consisted chiefly of young Black people.

The most well-known at the time were: *The British Black Panther Party (BPP), founded in 1969, The Black Liberation Front, founded 1971, The Black Freedom and Unity Party (BUFP), founded July, 1970, The Council For Afro-Asian Peoples (CAAP) , founded 1969, South East London Black Parents Association, founded in 1970. The Black Parents Movement and The Black Student Movement were founded in 1975.*

The Caribbean and American music - calypso, blues, ska, rocksteady and reggae and blues, jazz and soul provided the spiritual up-liftments of Black civil rights activists. In the Boxing World, Sunny Liston, Cassius Clay (Muhammad Ali), Joe Fraser, George Foreman, Leroy Spinks, Leon Spinks, Liverpool born, John Conteh, and others inspired Black people in Britain, with their powerful talents in the ring. *"Black And Proud"* was the slogan of the era. This boosted confidence among the Black poor. Television made it possible for members of the Black Community in Britain to witness people looking like them, gaining international respect and acclaim from various cultures.

It was noted that there was another type of change going on. That was China's Great Leaps, led by Chairman Mao Tse-tung. Mao led three major leaps - Political, Industrial and Cultural. His last leap was a Cultural Revolution with his Red Guards, as the youth of China made world news almost daily, in their making revolutionary changes to China's Society. In addition, What members of the British Black Community noted at the time was the Chinese willingness to offer to the Tanzanian Government the know-how to build a Railway at no extra cost, and that it would be built in record time, while the government of the West refused.

Fidel Castro and Che Guevara, both heroes of the Cuban Revolution, were making very important statements at the time. Guevara continued his revolutionary fight in Bulevia, where he lost his life. The Cubans inspired many Black people in Britain, not because they understood the theories of communism or socialism - the majority did not, but partly because they knew that a significant number of the Cubans were Africans, once made slave and now being able to fight as equals for important changes in their society.

The British Black Panther Party's leading lights were Edmond Lecointe, Dominican born, Keith Spencer, Jamaican born, Althea Jones-Lecointe, Trinidan born, David Udo, Nigerian born and Keith Francis, African born in the Caribbean.

On 31st August, 1970, at 10.30pm, Bank Holiday, the Black Panther Party organised a social function, at the Oval House, in Kensington, South London, at which 600 people were reported to be in attendance. Police from the Kensington, Brixton and Clapham North, stations, estimated by on-lookers to be 100 strong, entered the dance in its full swing, with a Caucasian women looking for an alleged Black youth who stole her watch and entered the social function earlier. The woman was unable to identify anyone in such a large group of people, and in any event, the women was reported to have remarked that " all Black people look alike."

That type of insensitive policing precipitated a pitch battle between the police and dancers in the Oval House. As a result, serious charges were laid by the police against the dance organisers. Keith Spencer was charged with riotous affray and grievous bodily harm; Althea Jones-Lecointe charged with incitement to riot, incitement to assault police, riotous affray, threatening behaviour, actual bodily harm and offensive weapon and Edmond (Eddie) Lecointe, with assault, bodily harm, and riotous affray and Keith Francis, with similar charges. This matter came to be known as *"The Oval Four"*.

The British Black Panther Party (BPP) approach to community development was based largely on pragmatism, with a socialist face. The following is a statement of what the Black Panther Party stood for at the time. This was published widely in the BPP's "Black People's News Service". As an historical record it is reproduced word for word accordingly:

"BLACK PANTHR MOVEMENT [14]
BLACK PANTHER MOVEMENT in Britain stands fundamentally for LIBERATION. Liberation of ALL oppressed people, and primarily the liberation of black people totally and from every form of enslavement and exploitation.

THE SITUATION OF BLACK PEOPLE IN BRITAIN

Why are we black people here in Britain in the first place ? We are in Britain not by choice or by chance, but because of the historical fact that Britain first came to our own countries.

Britain plundered and colonised our homelands with ruthless violence, subjected us to the most inhuman

84

torture and took us at gunpoint from Africa and Asia to the Caribbean and the Americas to build up wealth, exercising control over our natural resources by brutal force and swindle, and for 400 years now she has continued to pump the natural wealth of our different countries to provide a high standard of living for the people in this country, while our own people back home who produced the wealth, live in abject poverty and in most inhuman conditions.

In the early part of this century Britain caused widespread economic depression and hard living conditions for us in our different countries. Britain herself was then facing national disaster, industrial collapse and economic ruin as a result of the two World Wars. Britain therefore induced us in 'her colonies' to come to help in the building of her ruined industries.

Britain recruited us into her factories and firms for industrial production. Britain engaged our men and women to run her transport services and our nurses, midwives and doctors to maintain her health and medical services.

Thus Britain herself is responsible for our being in this country to provide the main labour force that keeps her industry going.

WHAT WE WANT

1   We want an immediate end to the racist immigration policies of the government. We want an end to the constant harassment at the ports of entry and the unwarranted detention in prison of black people by the racist immigration officials

2   We want an end to racism and exploitation in employment. Black people [must] be given employment as well as full pay in keeping with their

skill and experience. Black workers must organise to demand their right since British trade unions do not function in the interest of black people.

3   We want an end to racism and exploitation in housing operated against black people by the government and local councils. We demand an immediate end to the racket and intimidation practised by greedy landlords and estate agents against black people. We demand decent housing for black people instead of the present sub-standard houses in the slums of Britain. Black people have a right to make these demands, and it is the responsibility of the government and the local authorities to provide us with decent housing. Therefore, we black people, must organise ourselves into effective associations to see that these demands are met.

4   We demand an end to the brainwashing of our children in British schools and through the mass media. We demand proper education for all black people which will equip us with a true understanding of ourselves and which will expose the decadence of this white racist society. We want our people to learn the true history of black people which exposes the savage nature of colonial exploitation, since British education has purposely distorted our history and has 'glorified' the brutality of white exploiters who plundered our lands.

5   We demand an immediate end to police brutality and persecution of black people. We want an end to false arrest and imprisonment of black people. We want an end to the constant beating up, physical as well as mental torture of black people by prison offers.

We maintain that a government which fails to see these basic demands has no right whatever to claim or even expect our allegiance. And since the government with the entire capitalist establishment has not only failed to meet the demands but is directly responsible for the mounting racism, exploitation, brutality and degradation which black people suffer daily, then we have no alternative but to reject the entire racist capitalist establishment of Britain. This means in practice, first, we must stop building our hopes for a better future as black people on the empty hypocritical policies of the British government, whether Labour or Conservative. Secondly, we ourselves must bring about the change in our present oppressive situation right here in Britain. We must unite and get organised in order to defend ourselves in a racist and hostile society; and we must join with all other oppressed and revolutionary forces in Britain to fight for the complete overthrow of the oppressive capitalist system and for our liberation and that of all oppressed people.

WHAT WE DO IN PRACTICE

1. COMMUNITY WORK

Working among black people in the community, going from door to door, on the streets and in the markets as means of exchanging information about what happens to us in Britain.

2. BLACK HISTORY

Holding weekly studies and discussion on the history of black people

3. POLITICAL EDUCATION

Holding weekly classes and political education in order to have a better understanding of the racist capitalist system that oppress us, and in order to develop a correct analysis of our situation and a clear ideology towards our liberation.

4. CULTURAL ACTIVITIES

Organising activities to enable us to appreciate more fully the way of life of our people.

5. COURTS AND PRISONS

a   Attending courts in order to identify ourselves with any black person appearing for trial before the racist magistrates and judges of the British legal system.

b   Providing any possible assistance needed in the legal defence of black people

c   Keeping contact with black people in prison who are deliberately forced into isolation by the racist establishment.

6. BLACK CHILDREN

a   Providing extra lessons for black children who are often neglected and badly taught at school.

b   Organising activities for younger children on Saturday mornings to relieve the parents of some of the pressure of work at the weekend

7. PUBLIC MEETINGS

Organising public meetings and demonstrations on important issues that concern black people and all other oppressed people.

8. NEWS SERVICE

a   To keep black people constantly informed of what is happening to other black people.

b   To give black people the opportunity to express their views concerning our situation here in Britain and in other parts of the world

9. BOOKS AND LITERATURE

Providing books, magazine, posters, newspapers etc. on the history, political development and liberation struggle of black people in different parts of the world.

10.   Black Panther Movement undertakes these activities in practice because we believe it is not simply to talk about our problems. It is only when all of us black people are prepared to help ourselves and actively participate in activities such as these that we will make a meaningful move towards unity and ultimately towards our liberation.

SEIZE THE TIME !

ALL POWER TO THE PEOPLE !

SOLIDARITY IN THE STRUGGLE MEANS SHARING THE WORK OF THE SRUFGGLE."

The Leadership of The Black Liberation Front (BLF) operated *'GRASSROOTS'* [15], its Newspaper, which had notional readership. One of the leading lights was Tony Soares, who also edited *'GRASSROOTS'.*

The BLF was founded in January 1971 by the North London and Acton branches of the Black Panther Movement that split away after disagreement over policy. The BLF established and subsequently launched its Newspaper, *'GRASSROOTS'.*

By summer 1971, the BLF had established its youth league in North London, "The Black Berets" and opened a branch in the Shepherds Bush area of West London. BLF started a supplementary school and various other projects. BLF became "the UK chapter of the Revolutionary People's Communication network" linking the struggles of Black people all over the world.

In November 1971 and early 1972, the BLF was raided by Britain's Special Branch Police, because of an article that was re-printed in *'GRASSROOTS'* . The Editor was arrested. The Police raided again. Towards the end of 1972, the BLF and another pressure group called 'Fasimbas' merged into one, as BFL was loosing mass membership. BFL campaigned for the release of Tony Soares and the Oval 4, which arose out of the police entering the Oval House dance on 31 August, 1970.

BLF went through further reorganisation, as it "refined its ideology." The Organisation set out its new programme in a paper for discussion called "Revolutionary Black Nationalism", giving ideological guidelines.

The BLF participated in the 6th Pan African Congress and the Pan African Movement, and established an economic arm and social welfare arm to the organisation. BLF initiated a number of projects of concern to members of the Black Community, which included housing, employment, legal, and education.

In the following, BLF aims are reproduced word for word:

"AIMS

The BLF is struggling to:

1. End racist immigration laws
2. Stop police brutality and harassment
3. End discrimination in housing and employment
4. Seek justice for black people
5. Protect Black people from fascist attacks
6. Teach children our history and culture
7. End the oppression of Black women
8. Liberate our home countries. "

The BLF believed that the only methods by which Black people were going to free themselves were through "self-help and self-reliance". BLF active members were expected to do about three hours a week community work in one of BLF projects, and participate fully in making and implementing policy.

On the other hand, The Black Unity and Freedom Party (BUFP) held its first National Congress "of unity and new consciousness" on 20th July, 1970 "(being the commemorative day of the Cuban Revolution)". The Party was launched at the same time as "BLACK VOICE", "to carry articles explaining BUFP ideological and organisational position to readers". George Joseph, born in Trinidad, was a leading light in the BUFP.

"BLACK VOICE" was intended to carry on the work of *"THE WEST INDIAN GAZETTE"*, which stopped publishing in 1965 after the death of Claudia Jones, in December 1964. She was born in Trinidad and resided in England, and founded and Edited the *GAZETTE.*

BUFP published a Manifesto[16] at the same time of its launch, which outlined the Party's 'long term' and 'short-term' aims. BUFP developed its philosophy on Marxism apparently with a Maoist interpretation.

BUFP long-term programme is reproduced word for word below:

"BLACK UNITY AND FREEDOM PARTY
MANIFESTO LONG-TERM PROGRAMME

1   We recognise the class nature of this society.
2   We recognise the necessity for class struggle and the absolute necessity for the seizure of state power by the working class and the bringing about of socialism.
3   We recognise that imperialism has been able to inject its racist ideology into every section of society. However, since the white working class is also exploited under capitalism/imperialism, we recognise the contradiction between the white working class and the ruling class to be a fundamental one.

4   The contradiction between the black people and the ruling class is therefore a principal contradiction, and the contradiction between the black people and the white working class is only secondary.

5   Therefore, whilst we recognise the necessity to struggle against racism in general, it is essential to treat the contradiction between ourselves and the working class as a contradiction among the people, whilst the contradiction between ourselves and the ruling class is a contradiction between the people and the enemy.

6   The general programme of the party is therefore aimed at the complete overthrowing of capitalism/imperialism and towards bringing to an end the exploitation of man by man. The party,

therefore, upholds the right of the oppressed and the exploited everywhere to use any means necessary to free themselves from the yoke of capitalism/imperialism. We shall unite and fight with them to overthrow capitalism/imperialism.

B.U.F.P.
SHORT-TERM AIMS

WE DEMAND
1   We demand an immediate public enquiry into the brutal racist activities of the police against black people.
2   We demand an immediate end to the harassment of black people at the ports of entry by racist immigration officers.
3   We demand an immediate repeal of the Race Relations Act, since it is a tool to be used against black people.
4   We demand the scrapping of the Race Relations Board
5   We demand that all money paid into the various National Insurance and superannuation schemes be refunded to black people returning to their homelands.
6   We demand full employment for all black people.
7   We demand trial by our peers - i.e. black magistrates, judges and juries.
8   We demand the immediate release of all black people since they have not had a fair trial.
9   We demand an end to the racist education that is being dished out to our children. Black children must be taught their true history and culture by trained black people. Black parents must also have a greater control over their children's education. Therefore, in all schools where there are black children there must be a representative number of black people on the governing board.
10   We demand decent housing

11   We demand bread, peace and social justice for all men."

The Council for Afro-Asian Peoples (CAAP) was co-founded by Jamaican born Vince Hines, in 1969, in Paddington North West London. His co-founders were Philip C.D. York, born in St. Vincent, in the Caribbean, Fitzroy Hoffman, born in Jamaica, Neville Clare, born in Jamaica, Harsh Vadgama, born in India, Lloyd Timoll, born in Jamaica, Derrick Stemat, born in Jamaica, Hasmukh N Shah, born in Kenya, East Africa, Dayananda Perera, born in Ceylon (later called SriLanka), Ann Parris, born in the USA, Genevieve Umemju Ngbaronye, born in Nigerian/Biafra, West Africa, Grantley Mason, born in Barbados, Loretta Johnson, born in Jamaica, Chukwuemeka Ibegbuna, born in Nigerian, Lawrance Heroley, born in Guyana, South America, Gweneth Balson, born in Dominica, Caribbean, Coral Alder, born in Guyana and Mark Ashimi, born in Nigeria.

Excerpts from CAAP's inaugural press release read:

"In 1969 several young, self-disciplined, honest-minded and sensible Africans And Asians, some of whom are students, civil servants, accountants, bank clerks, airmen, engineers and nurses, got together and formed the Council For Afro-Asian Peoples.

 CAAP was formed not through emotions but reason: reason, because we realised that unless our realistic peoples got together and pool our resources (ideas, organising abilities, education and capital, etc.) a basically secure future for Afro-Asian Peoples living in Britain is not guaranteed.

We realise that what we were setting out to achieve was like attempting to bridge the River Thames, but we know that we had to achieve even the impossible, which demands consciousness, dedication and almost killing work.

Because we are individuals of different personalities and make-ups, we will ever have differences of opinions on certain issues. That is quite a natural thing. But we must not allow our antagonists to use our basic differences to divide us. Whatever the situation, WE MUST maintain linked arms.

It should be clearly understood that Afro-Asian peoples have no quarrels with honest, decent, sensible and humane whites in Britain. What black people are guarding against is racism.

On the other hand it must be equally understood that however well-intentioned our liberal whites are, they must not seek to lead blacks. CAAP should strongly discourage white leadership of Our People. We must make our own decisions. Those genuine whites who want to help us, should do so financially and technically, without laid down conditions.

On a larger scale, our white citizens who want to help blacks should spend their physical energy educating other whites on racial tolerance. It is clear that a section of the British population needs someone to help them understand Afro-Asian peoples. Else whites might continue to live in a 'civilised' world, suffering from nightmares and irrational anxieties injected into them by their racist colleagues.

The British people must be educated to understand that, when a black family moves into a white street, whites living on that street will not turn black - that nothing will necessarily change. Whites must be educated that their fears are unreal.

Unfortunately, however, the fears of our white citizens seem to grow daily, and in this case, we Afro-Asian peoples must rigidly maintain our Black Consciousness, keeping our arms tightly linked in our *Togetherness* for our survival. No Afro-Asian man, woman, or child should forget the racially grave time in which we live.

THE TIME MUST BE CONSIDERED. "

CAAP operated a Newsletter and the following is a word for word production of the Council's plan of action published in February, 1970:

"THE COUCIL FOR AFRO-ASIAN PEOPLES
- NEWS LETTER (SUPPLEMENT)[17]
A REMINDER OF CAAP'S PROGRAMME
HONESTY, DISCIPLINE AND SELF-RESPECT ARE OUR BASE"

INTRODUCTION:

The following are partly extracts from the Constitution of The Council For Afro-Asian Peoples, compiled for the benefit of our members and friends. The information below shows what we in CAAP have dedicated our services to do for OUR PEOPLES in the United Kingdom, chiefly because of necessity and because of the almost "grave" period in which we are living. The functions are triangular: Economic, Political and Social.

ECONOMIC:

1. a)   CAAP aims to provide the expertise necessary for the successful working of co-operative movement in given areas - areas where co-ops are likely to succeed.
   b)   To provide the expertise necessary for the successful working of private companies

c) To invest in real estate in order to help to provide good housing facilities for OUR PEOPLES. As we are aware, the acute housing situation is becoming a pressing and growing problem, which we must face.

d) The above economic foundation should ensure certain basic growing economic roots for OUR PEOPLES in the United Kingdom. Afro-Asian Economic foundation in the U.K. is obviously vital, and that foundation must be a JOINT ONE, because jointly, we should be able to withstand economic pressures.

POLITICAL:
2. a)   CAAP aims to provide a firm political foundation upon which Afro-Asian citizens will stand and put certain necessary pressures to bear on Society - in other words, CAAP is positioning itself at a point at which, when it speaks, agitating for better jobs, housing, etc. for OUR PEOPLES, CAAP's voice will be heard in the right quarters to bring about changes.

b) To expose more fully Police brutality - to OUR CHILDREN in particular and to OUR PEOPLE in general - to the light of justice. Such illegal Police action must be stopped !

c) To provide a strong Legal Panel to advise members on legal matters.

d)   To organise OUR PEOPLES in factories in order to overcome bad working conditions and low wages, thus forming where necessary Afro-Asian Workers' Association and co-ordinate closely with corresponding Afro-Asian Bodies, and European (White) unions. This will help to ensure that the interest of Afro-Asian Workers are protected.

e) To investigate complaints of discrimination - among others- of Afro-Asian doctors and nurses in British Hospitals.

f) To link arms with Afro-Asian Organisations in the United Kingdom and in OUR MOTHER COUNTRIES, that is, India, Africa, Pakistan, The West Indies, and so on.

g) To provide Afro-Asian candidates to contest local government elections, by-elections, and general election in given Afro-Asian populated areas in the United Kingdom.

SOCIAL:

3. a) CAAP aims to provide entertainment facilities for members - facilities for parties, dances, shows, etc.

b) SPORTS. To provide facilities for games: cricket, football, badminton, squash, hockey, table-tennis, judo, dominoes, etc.

c) To provide facilities to encourage our members to visit our Mother Countries - flights to: India, Africa, Pakistan, the West Indies and so on. Also to provide other travelling facilities for outings - coach trips, and other general travelling arrangements as required.

d) ART AND CULTURE. To encourage members to take active interests in our ancestors' arts and cultural patterns, in order to maintain our identities, living in a Society of which the majority of whose members are of a different history, tradition, custom, morality, and cultural background. To help to effect this, CAAP will support an Afro-Asian University, and if necessary, open one of OUR OWN in the long run.

e) Visit our sick and imprisoned members

f) To provide where necessary, nurseries, play fields and homes for OUR CHILDREN.

g) To provide Youth Clubs for OUR ever increasing number of YOUTH.

h) To provide convalescent facilities for members.

i) To provide facilities to care for OUR OLD (and respected) PEOPLES.

j) To take care of our members' funeral rites for those dependants who need it.

IN ADDITION - COMMUNICATION:

CAAP aims to provide an Afro-Asian National Press to supply OUR PEOPLES with local, national and international information - information presently unobtainable in our British media: Press, Radio and Television. The Afro-Asian Press will publish information chiefly of the activities of Afro-Asian Peoples in the United Kingdom and abroad, and will provide OUR PEOPLES with what THEY WANT to read, dealing with social, economic, political and relevant matters."

By 1975, the formation of The Black Parents And Black Students Organisations was an indication of entrench police malpractice, supported largely by the courts, particularly the magistrates courts at the time. The members of the Black Parents' Movement (BPM) And The Black Students' Movement (BSM), whose leading light was Trinidad born John LaRose, focussed their work on community development, enabling and empowering members of the Black Community, particularly families who were at a lost to understand the British judiciary and the education system.

The BPM and BSM were involved, particularly in the North London area, in organising unemployed youth, students and parents in the West Indian community into a force capable of waging a struggle against police oppression and the legal system

The following represents the position of the BPM and The BSM during 1975:[18]

"WHERE WE STAND
The BPM and BSM took a stand against the community relations organisations, the Community Relations Commission, the Community Relations industry. The stand which the BPM takes is, that the Community Relations organisation, the Community Relations industry is a kind of colonial office for the black community in this country, which seek to undermine the independent organisational activity of the black population in dealing with its own struggles.

We believe - at this important period where the black working class faces strikes, unemployment in the railway and the Post Office, where the youth and older black working class is in constant conflict with the police and education authorities, with the State at every level, through individual acts of oppression - that we suffer, through this capitalist system of oppression, and that at this particular moment, it has become necessary to clarify for ourselves where we are going and how we intend to go about what we are trying to do.

We stand for the independent, black, radical and revolutionary organisation of Black people. We stand for that and we also stand for linking our struggles with other groups in the society - linking our struggles together and working out our ideological position as we link our struggles together.

We see the country today as a country of nationalists - the English, the Scots, the Welsh, the Irish, the Greeks, and Blacks and the Asians, which would also include the Indians, the Pakistani, the Bangladeshis. And we know that inside each of these nationalities, there is an internal struggle that takes place between the oppressed section of that group and those who are prepared to use the State against the interest of those who are oppressed

A significant portion of the work of BPM and BSM dealt with community legal defence work - taking defendants' statement, assisting the same to select, test and tried competent solicitors and lawyers for defence, and accompany defendants to courts. BPM and BSM informed members of the wider public of charges and cases against Black youth appearance in court. BPM and BSM prepared and published leaflets and distribute the same to members of the public, calling attention to the injustice against members of the Black Community, where they existed. There was an insistence that defendants should have an important say in their defence and that defending lawyers should listen to defendants' instructions.

BPM and BSM were based in the North of London, and supported defendants in cases like the Harlesden 6, Black women who were beaten up in Harlesden outside the Burning Spear Club, in North London , the Woodgreen 18 and Cliff McDaniel of the Black Youth Movement.

By 1970, the South East London Parent Organisation (SELPO), lead by George Campbell, Jamaican born, emphasis was placed on the education of the Black child in the education system and the new immigration laws proposed by the Labour Government, which would restrict dependants coming to join families. SELPO organisation focussed its attention in this area, including support for youth activities, which would lead inevitably to setting up legal defence groups for the stream of youth being brought by the police before the courts.

SEPLO found that most of the convictions that Black youth had, they received at the hands of magistrates courts, that was also known as Police Courts. Many of SEPLO members believed at the time that some magistrates courts were rubber stamps for the police actions against members of the Black Community.

Out of SEPLO came the *FASIMBAS*, a successful Black nationalist organisation, whose members were mostly Black youth. *FASIMBAS* was formed as a defence against police malpractice against members of the Black Community in the local area. In 1971, the *FASIMBAS* amalgamated with The Black Liberation Front.

The North London West Indian Association (NLWIA)[19] was one of the West Indian Committees amalgamated to form the West Indian Standing Conference in 1959. NLWIA operated in the London Borough of Haringey and had an impressive record in campaigning for the rights of Black workers and Black children. NLWIA attracted membership from immigrants recruited from the Caribbean to work for London Transport. Others were factory and hospital workers.

In April 1968 NLWIA took on London Transport (LT) and mounted a picket outside of LT Headquarters, in protests against lack of promotion for Black workers. At the time NLWIA accused both LT and the Transport and General Workers Union of collusion in holding back promotion of Black workers.

NLWIA demands - promotion for Black bus crew and LT acceptance of Lionel Franklin for training to become a Bus Inspector - were won. NLWIA members were prepared to go on strike if it was necessary. Jeff Crawford and Ralf Straker, both born in Barbados, had been two of the guiding lights of NLWIA. As a result of West Indian children being wrongly placed in Educational Sub-normal schools in August 1968, NLWIA set up the Paul Bogle Youth Club, independent of the local authorities to give support to Black children in need.

10.   Black People And The Police In England 1950-1975

THE 1824 VAGRANCY ACT, SECTION 4, CONTRIBUTED TO CIVIL UNRESTS among members of the Black Community and the Police during the 1970s and 80s, particularly among Black youth, who were invariably charged with "being a suspected person loitering with intent to commit an arrestable offence contrary to section 4 of the Vagrancy Act, 1924." (see reference note 9).

This was commonly known as the 'sus law' by members of the Black Community, partly because the charge referred to a person acting 'suspiciously' with intent to commit a crime. Charges for carrying fire arms and possession of, or using,   Class A drugs were very rare, at this era of Black Community development. The Police often used the 'sus law' to harass and criminalise Black youth. This created bad feelings among the youth, which subsequently led to serious and dramatic civil unrests in Britan's inner cities.

Black people (and their White sympathisers), Black youth in particular, complained bitterly about police harassment, and set up organisations to put a stop to that harassment.

Andrea Shervington, a 47 year old Guyanese, living in Notting Hill Gate during 1970, [20]came to Britain in 1950. He explained: "I can remember in 1950 when the exodus of Black people started arriving in Britain to fill the 'Mother Country's' labour gap, left by the 'war of liberation'. We had our minor tiffs with the police, but never anything in the line of race - usually matters rose out of our attitudes, being a gay people.

"The noises we made on the buses and trains, the parties we held, and so on. Soon things changed, when we began to own properties, like cars and homes. It was then that we noticed the police repression.

"The police often saw four of us in a car and automatically assumed that the car was stolen. Should the car contain a White girl, the police tended to be more offensive. We were invariably taken to a police station and questioned about our car," said Andrea.

The situation between the Police and members of the Black community deteriorated. In 1969, the First Secretary of the Nigerian High Commission in London was "brutally beaten by the police in Brixton, South East London." The Diplomat was driving a white Mercedes Benz at the time. At the Brixton police station, the identity of the First Secretary was discovered, but it was too late. The arresting officers "assumed the Nigerian stole the car".

Rudy Narayan, an Indian Barrister at Law in London, born in Guyana, and deeply involved in helping to keep Black people out of British jails, explained: "The Black man in Britain has got to be a 'criminal or violent'. To divert from that set pattern, he will be harassed and even crushed by the police. If Black people showed that they have pride, and stand up against repression, the police will find ways of charging them with obstruction, assault and/or insulting behaviour.

" There is a general assumption by the police of guilt of imaginary crimes, whenever they see Black people gathering in threes or fours in the streets. There is also an assumption of helplessness. The police believe that they can pull up Black people any time, any how, without having to account for their actions.

"I handled a case recently," Rudy continued, "of one Mr. St. Louis, living in Islington, London. He suffered four broken ribs, intense bleeding and vomiting while in police custody. The case was sent to the police Commissioner and he replied that there was not enough evidence to warrant a prosecution against the police officers who attacked my client.

"If this society was a just one, the police would not have the powers they now have. But this society is one of inequalities and struggles, which uses the police as instrument of repression," Rudy concluded. (See reference notes 20)

A Seminar was held at the West Indian Student Centre in Collingham Gardens, South West London, on 27 September, 1970, to discuss 'the deteriorating relationships, the growing mistrust and lack of confidence, between Black people and the Police'.

West Indian Students in the United Kingdom thought that 'A solution was absolutely necessary if peaceful community relations are to exist'. The Seminar was chaired by Mr D. S. Chung, and speakers were Gary Burton, born in Antigua, President of the West Indian Student Union, Jeff Crawford, born in Barbados, General Secretary of the West Indian Standing Conference, Rudy Narayan, Jonathan Guinness, Caucasian, of the Monday Club, John Lambert, Senior Research Associate for Urban and Regional Studies, Birmingham University and Inspector Reg. Gale, Chairman of the Police Federation. Inspector Gale said: [1] "It is difficult to argue that we are not agents of the Establishment. But we do not make the

---

[1] See Britain, The Black Man, And The Future, page 17, in reference note 20

laws that we have to enforce. They are made by people that you never see.

"I see the whole problem as a social one, and I don't know what the answer is. I am quite content to have an independent element in the present complaint procedure [of the police] to make the public satisfied".

Inspector Gale continued: "I do not believe that all policemen are perfect. We try to cure their imperfections if there are any. But you cannot blame the police for lack of government leadership. You cannot blame the police for carrying out their jobs."

The gulf between the Police and members of the Black Community widened, which led to mass demonstrations in major English cities by Black people against police repression.

This resulted in one of many clashes between members of the Police and the Black Community on August 1970 during a demonstration in Notting Hill Gate against "police brutality of Black people". The clashed happened at Portland Road.[21] Thirty Black people were charged with incitement to riot, assault on police, and affray. One man, Roddy Kentish, born in Jamaica, was charged with attempted murder of a police officer, "who fainted during the heat of the arrest".

Evon, a 17-year-old Black girl, one of the thirty charged, complained of police attacks on her. She was arrested for allegedly assaulting police offers. She was then taken to Harrow Road Police Station, in West London and "beaten" [2]

"I was slapped, kicked and punched," said Evon, "and I screamed MURDER!, which embarrassed my attackers

---

[2] See Britain, The Black Man And The Future, page 19, in reference note 20

who abruptly stopped beating me. That was upstairs. I understand later that people could hear my screams downstairs, including the person who came to bail me," Evon said.

Complaints of police malpractice were extensive during the 1970s and 1980s. The BBC Television programme "Cause for Concern", broadcast in August, 1968, documented cases where appeals against convictions of members of the Black Community were upheld, and examples of police malpractice shown up: planted evidence, perjured statements in court, and trumped-up charges. The facts were there. That was in 1968.

A spokesman for the Metropolitan Police at Scotland Yard explained: "The police have made genuine attempts to remedy these complaints by setting up a Community Relations Division and Liaison Officers in local immigrant areas."

He continued: "The police treat Black and White people alike. When approached by the police, Black youth tend to be arrogant and argumentative, asserting their rights. I agree that it is at that point the man on the beat is called upon to judge his client. Unless he is well-trained in Race Relations, his judgement is in danger of being clouded by his prejudices."

Leroy, a 17 year-old Black youth explained angrily: "If they continue to harass us, there may be open warfare. I have no intention of looking forward to a future of police harassment. The police are making life very difficult for Black people and their sympathisers, because they know that if we got together and become one, the shouts of the exploited and oppressed will become unified.

"We have been reminded time and time again that Black people are a minority group in Britain, but I believe that we have a lot of White friends who will stand by us - people who believe in humanity and justice," Leroy said.

Leroy continued: "The police actions against the community, in the ghettos in particular, are illegal to the citizens, but legal to the police. The police seem to be enforcing their OWN laws. I was sent 'inside' through police trumped-up charges, of obstruction and threatening behaviour. The policeman who trumped up my charges told me that I was to plead guilty in court, and promised that he would put in a 'good word' for me with the presiding magistrate. I said NO.

"I was certain that I would get off, since I was innocent, but the magistrate sent me down. Now I don't expect justice from the magistrates courts anymore. I have already made up my mind to go to prison. But no prison will kill my will to be free," Leroy said.

Inspector Reg. Gale of the Police Federation, was informed at the West Indian Students' Centre by a speaker from the very angry crowd who said: "When the wrath of the Black Community erupted, when Black people felt that they have had enough harassment and injustices from the police, they roar and behave like lions. We feel very strongly about the way the British police have been harassing and brutalising our Black youth and adults," the speaker concluded.

Frank Critchlow, born in Trinidad, and owner of the Mangrove Restaurant, based in Ladbroke Grove, West London, explained: "To me, what we are dealing with in society is not a social question, nor a mere question of the police, but we are dealing with a thorny political problem, and the only solution for the MINE situation with the police is that it is the Police Federation's responsibility to see that its members' actions, and what they are doing to members of the Black Community are not done. It is the responsibility of the government to see that the Federation carries that out."

Frank continued: "That is Black people's position. beyond that there can be no dialogue. The tempo of the Black Community is steadily rising. We are now at a position of looking to see what the authorities are doing about police control. It is also the responsibility of the entire British population to see that Black people are not molested and interfered with by policemen. If the people failed to stand up and be counted, then they too become the oppressors," Frank said.

11. POLICE/WEST INDIAN IMMIGRANT RELATIONSHIPS

Joint Conference Between England And Wales Police Federation, Caribbean High Commissions And West Indian Community Leaders, London - 28th November 1970

By 1970, the relationship between the West Indians and the Police was at a critical stage, to the extent that The Police Federation of England And Wales initiated a conference in co-operation with the Caribbean High Commissions and the Commission for the Associated States of the West Indies, on "Police/West Indian Immigrant Relationships" which was held at the Commonwealth Institute on Saturday 28th November, 1970[22].

The Conference was attended by senior members of the Caribbean diplomatic service, including High Commissioners, senior members of the Police Federation and West Indian Community Leaders. The holding of this Conference was unprecedented in the British law enforcement history, which demonstrated the strengths and impact of the African Caribbean Community protest against social repression.

The primary objective of the Conference was to stimulate a positive and continuing dialogue between the Police and grassroots level of the West Indian Immigrant community. It had been recognised and accepted by both sides that the greatest areas of conflict laid between the lower echelons of the Police establishment and the immigrant community and that to enable the processes of education and understanding to make any meaningful impact upon the existing unsatisfactory situation in order to disperse the miasma of suspicion that existed on both sides, efforts would have to be directed towards setting the right basis for the machinery of dialogue, consultation and discussion to move smoothly and uninterruptedly between the Police and West Indian Immigrants.

PART ONE: REPORT ON CONFERENCE, 28th November, 1970

SURVEY OF POLICE/WEST INDIAN IMMIGANT RELATIONSHIPS IN THE UNITED KINGDOM 1970. *(Full Text Of The Paper Presented By A.E.Alberga, Legal Attaché, Jamaican High Commission, London, For The High Commissions Of The Caribbean And The People They Represent, Who Are Residents Of The United Kingdom).*

The United Kingdom is now a multi-racial state. This term seems to be used today to describe any society with non-white persons. At present, the United Kingdom is well on its way to being the most cosmopolitan society in the world, even more so than the United States, France, Holland, Canada, Central and South America and even the West Indies.

Is this a step forward, as some people think, or is it a portent of doom as others forecast ? History does not provide an answer despite reference to older and more mature multi-racial societies. What seems certain is that the answer to the questionable social future of Britain lies with the people living within its confines.

No reference to other societies can provide a satisfactory prognosis as conditions vary from place to place and different effects result from the various causes peculiar to each society.

Let us dispassionately attempt to examine the present state of the social situation in the United Kingdom to see whether the presence of non-white foreshadows doom or represents a forward step.

Firstly, we cannot accept that the intermingling of races automatically produces conflict. This is a doctrine propounded by South Africa that has, as its basis, a religious creed. Apart from this doubtful interpretation of biblical passages, there is nothing to suggest that black and white cannot live harmoniously together.

In any case, South Africa cannot truly be called multi-racial. We must, therefore, look for other reasons why there has been conflict between black and white in so called multi-racial societies. The society usually cited in support of this conflict theory is the United States of America. There we see the struggle black people have been waging for over three hundred years to participate in a society which constitutionally gives them equal rights with other members of the society. The blacks in that society, like the blacks in Central and South America and the Caribbean area, commenced life in the New World with the status of slaves. Like the Greeks, Turks, Anglo Saxons and other Europeans, who were once enslaved by the Romans, the blacks from the Caribbean, Central and South America shrugged off the status and lived once more like free men sharing the ultimate benefits offered by their own societies. The struggle of the American blacks has taken a longer time and has been more violent due no doubt to the reluctance of his white brothers to share the wealth of that great society.

Unlike the United Kingdom, other mainly white societies (e.g. France, Holland, Canada) have absorbed black immigrants with little fuss. Even the United States have invited the black immigrants to reside there permanently. What is significant is the status of these immigrants. They are all free persons, unlike their forebears who had been taken against their will. Why then should there be this mental disquiet in the United Kingdom over the presence of non-white persons ?

After all, the Italians today bear no grudge against their former slaves and the British have often boasted to the world that they had the best empire the world had ever seen. They often said that the British taught the world justice and fair play and had humanised the black world which made up a great portion of its empire. Why then should this civilised mass of humanity still be rejected after some thirty years of residence in the British society ?

Some might argue that there is no rejection because the society now consists of nearly two million Asians and West Indians legally within its midst. Legally - because Parliament, the constitutionally supreme organ of the United Kingdom, has often stated that those who are here must be treated like first class citizens. Like the United States, therefore, the supreme constitutional body has declared its intention to create and/or maintain a stable and harmonious society which can only emerge if all persons within it are given every opportunity to participate without discrimination. But there is no acceptance either.

Parliament, despite its declaration of good intent, has had to pass a Race Relations Act in an attempt to persuade a section of the community that the harmony and stability of the society could only survive if everyone felt free to utilise the freedoms offered by the society. This Act has had some effect and there is overt improvement in some areas of the community. There is one situation, however, that has worsened steadily despite Parliament's declaration and enactment. I refer

114

to the heightening tension in the relationship between the police and the non-white community.

The police force in any country has serious responsibilities. Its members have obligations, not only to its official superiors, but also, and even more so, to the community it serves. Among its principal functions is the preservation of law and order. This embraces the prevention as well as the detection of crime. In fact, if there were no crime this would not be an indictment against, but a credit, to the force.

It is said that acrimony exists between the police force and the lowest stratum of every society. There is also a presumption that more criminals emerge from this group. Here in the United Kingdom, there appears to be an assumption that all non-whites belong to this lowest social group. Some whites from this group even attempt to create a sub group to categorise the non-whites. Most West Indians find this somewhat amusing and are prepared to challenge these assumptions. What they find difficult to understand is the apparent acceptance of this classification by some of the police force. The actions of this body suggest that it believes that the West Indians are in fact potential criminals. This attitude in the United States gave birth to extremist reaction in the black sector and there are some signs of a similar pattern here. Over the years, West Indians living in the U.K., those representing their Governments, have been resisting the constant feeling that there is a police campaign waged unfairly against the non-white sections of this community. This is a feeling never before experienced by West Indians in their long history of migration to other mainly white societies.

In 1969, some two hundred and forty (240) cases came to my attention of Jamaicans charged with certain offences. They were varied but it was conspicuous that some offences occurred frequently. Of these there were

21 charged with living on immoral earnings; 20 charged with being suspected persons; 24 charged with possession of drugs; 21 charged with assaulting the police; 16 with possessing offensive weapons and 7 charged with insulting and threatening behaviour. In 1970, 13 charges of assaulting police; 15 charges of possession of dangerous drugs; 8 cases of living on immoral earnings; 4 cases of possession of offensive weapons have emerged out of the 145 cases that have so far come to my attention.

Now we are well aware of the danger of using statistics to make a point. The figures quoted tell many stories, depending on what one is looking for, but I have cited these offences because I have had complaints from many Jamaicans of the haste of certain policemen in charging them with these offences. It is useful at this point to say that in Jamaica, with the exception of living on immoral earnings (virtually unknown there as an event) all the others are proscribed. All, except possession of dangerous drugs, these offences are not frequent in Jamaica.

Why, then, have these become popular in the U.K? This must be looked at seriously if there is to be a frank and open discussion of the situation. It is my considered opinion that the police are dangerously close to stereotyping the non-white sector. As a result, more and more members of the force have become contaminated by myths which have little or no basis. In my six years of involvement with the police and West Indian relationship in the U.K. I have heard many stories and seen incidents at first hand. Not all the stories may be true but my training has taught me to assess situations with some common sense and a degree of objectivity.

Police officers have told me that West Indians are assumed to be violent and so must be approached with force. Police officers have, on more than one occasion, been heard to summon other police officers by walkie talkie [police radio], merely by saying that there is a 'coloured' [Black] involve. There are frequent reports, and I have experienced this myself, of a refusal of an investigating officer to listen to a coloured person's account of an incident, particularly pronounced when there is an issue involving a coloured and a white (whether British or not). This has resulted in precipitate arrests of coloured persons accompanied by physical assaults, or threatened assaults, on these persons. In addition, there are many reports of verbal abuse like "why don't you people go home". "You black bastards don't know how to behave". "If this were South Africa you would be shot", and similar statements tending to illustrate the hidden venom nurtured by some police officers towards the non-white sector of this civilised society.

Where do we go from there ? The judicial process requires the arrested person to be taken before a Magistrate. At this point, the arrested person hopes to be vindicated as he has been taught, as part of the civilised teaching, that the Courts dispense justice. At this point it is useful to look again at the list of crimes which I contend is most common among the West Indian sector. All of these crimes are triable before a lay Magistrate in what used to be called police courts, now renamed Magistrates Court.

The evidence of one police officer is all that is required to secure a conviction in these Courts. (This standard of proof also operates before higher tribunals but in the presence of a jury where it is more microscopically examined). After visiting many Magistrates Courts in this country I can say with confidence that the attitude of the Magistrates is to accept the evidence of the police officer unless the prisoner can prove his innocence. This runs counter to all taught legal principles. The West Indian accused is in a poor situation in that he has got to convince the Magistrate that the police officer had no good reason to arrest him in the first place.

He cannot mention colour prejudice because, even if he is right, the Magistrate will say that that is imagined and irrelevant. He is therefore left to deal with the heavy burden of cross-examining the police officer, a trained witness, to show that he is not telling the truth. If, as sometimes happens, another West Indian gives evidence for the accused, the testimony is regarded as biased, even if the two persons never knew each other.

The evidence of a white person in similar circumstances is not so regarded and the scales are somewhat balanced. On this subject it is interesting to note that a white witness giving evidence for a white accused is not labelled biased if the witness does not know the accused beforehand.

These are the observations made over a period of years. A Magistrate once told me that she was told that, in the West Indies, the people are against policemen and therefore anything said by them in these Courts about the treatment by police officers here was taken with a grain of salt. She also thought that a police officer would not arrest a man unless he had done something wrong. This is the sort of naivety which encourages some police officers to tell any plausible story which they know will be believed by a Court.

Where I come from, a police officer's testimony is treated like that of anybody else's and there is no judicial restraint placed on the defence to test his evidence by intense cross-examination. Tribunals there observe the text book in the investigation of evidence. There is no judicial disapproval of a strong and proper cross-examination of a police witness if that is necessary to elicit the truth. As long as judges here express their disapproval of searching cross-examination of prosecution witnesses which contains allegations of relevant fact; as long as West Indians have reason to feel that they are harassed and then persecuted, as long as the complaints to proper channels go unheeded, as long as the public is unaware of this silent suffering, then the future of this multi-racial society is not difficult to foretell.

So far, institutions like the various High Commissions have tried to keep the dialogue going between the police and West Indians. I have personally found the police hierarchy sympathetic, understanding and sincere in their hope for better relations. Despite this, however, there were some in the ranks who have not kept faith and continue to anger the West Indians sector of the community.

The result is that West Indians doubt our ability in these representations and are losing faith in the established procedure for discussing grievances. We have taken great pains to sift the many complaint we receive about police behaviour, and we select and submit the ones we find most weighty and deserving of serious consideration. Despite this selectivity, on our part, not one complaint has ever been found justifiable by the police enquiry. Three possible alternatives flow from the investigation of a complaint.

- Firstly, if the complaint reveals possible criminal action on the part of the police officer he may be charged on the advice of the Director of Public Prosecution (an authority independent of the police).

- The second possibility is a charge against the officer as provided for by the Police Code of Discipline. The complainant is invited to attend these proceedings and they may be allowed to question the officer charged. As far as we know, no West Indian complainant has ever been invited to any such proceedings.

- The third course is that the complaint is unjustifiable. Over the past years all our representations have resulted in findings of no justification in the complaints. Recently, we have made this fact known to the Home Secretary for him to consider and record, in the light of the increasing clamour for independent investigation of complaints.

Whether or not it is the intention of the police, a climate of fear and distrust now operates within the West Indian sector. These, as we well know, are dangerous emotions, which can be transformed into more serious attitudes. Some West Indians are reluctant to walk or drive after dust, to visit public places or even gather at private homes where unwarranted entry by some police officers is commonplace. The American pattern of aborting black associations and harassing articulate leaders who advocate nothing more than human rights is now with us in this country. What is frightening is that the general public continues to regard the police as near perfect in the light of its public image of helping old persons and its personification of politeness. To some extent, this is understandable because the majority of persons do not experience the perfidy of the few who are basking in the image created by the many right thinking members of the force.

Consequently, the majority of the public regard the protestations of the black community as hysterical and do not display any sympathy as jurors in trials of non-white persons or participate at protest level. The press remain aloof and in that sense abdicate their responsibilities. With all such outlets closed, the non-white sector will inevitably employ other expressions of protest. This we know, is undesirable and we can only hope that this stage is never reached.

If it is the intention of some police officers to drive the West Indians out of the United Kingdom, I am afraid that they will not succeed by being instrumental in the convictions of innocent persons. In the case of West Indians, there is a history of migration that defies pressure of this kind. Even if West Indians decide to leave the U.K. for more agreeable climes, like Canada and the United States, those with [criminal] convictions are barred from entering those countries. As a consequence, they will either return to their homeland or remain in the United Kingdom.

Majority will remain here and it makes little sense to create a situation where they are bitter against the persons who prevented them from leaving to improve themselves. Even those who return home because of the pressure here carry with them a bitter taste and this can only spread the bigotry to areas where it had never existed before. In other words, some West Indians say that they learnt about race prejudice and discrimination in the United Kingdom and British people living in the West Indies are beginning to see the disastrous effects these have had on the minds of returning West Indians. The attitude of some police officers is therefore counter productive as far as British interests are concerned.

We are therefore hopeful that this conference will be meaningful, not so much in the promise we make, but in the action we take. Results cannot come too soon. The bitterness that is enveloping the West Indians sector ultimately will affect the society as a whole as the experience in the United States has shown. It is imperative that the police disabuse their minds of the prevailing myths and try to understand the West Indian. We would suggest that they understand:

1) That the West Indian community is just as stratified socially as the British community;

2) That the West Indian community is not here to cause trouble but to earn its living in the same way that British immigrants do all over the world

3) That the West Indian community has long since been rid of slavery; and the belief that he is just as good as the next man is enshrined in the West Indian's way of life;

4) That the West Indian community is not in the majority a drug taking one nor is it rude or violent unless its rights as human beings are threatened;

5) That members of the West Indian community have settled successfully in other parts of the world, mainly North, South and Central America without despoiling or contaminating these societies, and its reputation has always been good;

6) That there is nothing frightening about the ambition of the West Indian community because it wishes to improve itself economically in line with every other community in the U.K.; and

7) That the West Indian community is prepared to alter some of its social behaviour patterns which do not conform to the society in which it lives if there is a willingness on the part of the indigenous community to talk with it instead of persecuting it for transporting its domestic culture. In particular, I refer to loud music and expressive behaviour.

Policemen are not sociologists but they ought to understand that Britain had been changing ever since the second World War ended. Masses of refugees, far outnumbered the blacks [Black people] now in this society, came here with their culture and have been assimilated. The Jews with their style of dress and worship, the Italians, Germans, Irish, (all at one time or another engaged in hostilities with the British) have been assimilated. Eastern Europeans come here with little fuss, but traditional friends from the Caribbean are treated differently.

Before certain elements in the police force cause an irreversible situation, we would recommend that the police (especially those in plain clothes) be urged not to rock the boat.

We feel that the way towards building or maintaining a harmonious society is understanding. We should like to see fear, distrust, hatred eliminated, or at least minimised. There should be no reason why a police officer should not approach and converse with a West Indian in quite the same way that he confronts the average white person in the society.

It is only when the West Indian believes in the sincerity and experiences the civility of the police force will he be prepared to support the force in its endeavours. West Indians, deprecate criminal behaviour just as much as any other group and are just as anxious to assist when they can. Continued tension, however, between the two groups can be nothing but counter productive and produces conflicts which the society can do without. West Indians do not ask for special treatment as some police officers mistakenly believe; we ask for equal treatment as is our right.

We, on our part, undertake to guide the West Indian sector on the aspects which give most concern to the police. In our desire to improve the situation, we will continue to make every effort to reach West Indians throughout the country and instruct them on the social aberrations which seem to offend the community in general and the police force in particular.

REPORT: Part Two - Conference Proceedings And Resolutions

It was agreed that a moderate size Conference with representation from a wide cross section of the West Indian Immigrant community, coming from the various cities and towns in England, would provide this basic machinery for the beginning of the dialogue. Eighty participants and several representatives of the West Indian High Commissions and the Commission for the Eastern Caribbean Governments and seven members of the Police Federation took part in the Conference.

The Conference was presided over by the High Commissioner for Jamaica, Sir Laurence Lindo, who opened the proceedings by introducing the High Commissioners from Trinidad and Tobago, Guyana, Barbados, Mr N.G.F. Taylor, Commissioner for the Eastern Caribbean Governments, and Mr Reg. F.Gale, Chairman of the Central Committee of the Police Federation and the other members of his team to the participants.

Mr Gale explained briefly how the idea of the Conference originated, stated its aims and purpose, and outlined the agenda for the day. Mr Gale emphasised how important it was for participants to maintain a sense of proportion and offer constructive contributions to the discussions so that the aim for which the Conference was organised could be achieved.

The Conference Chair introduced Mr Allan E. Alberga, Legal Attaché of the Jamaican High Commission, who presented a paper, "Survey of Police - West Indian Immigrant Relationships In The United Kingdom Today".

In his paper, Mr Alberga gave a brief analysis of the attitudes which have dictated the status and treatment accorded to non-white citizens in countries in other parts of the world and compared these with the present status of non-white citizens in multi-racial Britain.

Mr Alberga spoke of the heightening tension in the relationship between the police and the non-white community, of a climate of fear and distrust of the Police amongst the West Indian sector of the community and illustrated these with examples of complaints which had been reported to him personally by Jamaicans. He spoke about the reluctance of the West Indians to walk or drive after dusk to visit public places or gather in private homes where unwarranted entry by some police offers was commonplace. "The American pattern of aborting black associations and harassing articulate leaders who advocate nothing more than human rights is now with us in Britain" he said.

Mr. Alberga made reference to frequent reports of a refusal of an investigating Police Officer to listen to a coloured [Black] person's account of an incident, particularly pronounced when there was an issue involving a coloured [Black] and a white person. These had resulted in precipitate arrests of coloured [Black] persons accompanied sometimes by physical assaults or threatened assaults on them.

Referring to Magistrates Courts' procedures, Mr Alberga said that from his own personal experience of their operations, he could say with confidence that the attitude of the Magistrates was to accept the evidence of the police officer unless the prisoner could prove his innocence. "The West Indian accused was in a poor situation in that he has to convince the Magistrates that the Police Officer had no good reason to arrest him in the first place. He cannot mention colour prejudice because even if he is right, the Magistrate will say that

that is imagined and irrelevant. He is therefore left to deal with the heavy burden of cross examining the police officer, a trained witness, to show that he is not telling the truth".

Institutions like the Caribbean High Commissions have attempted to keep the dialogue going between the Police and the West Indians. Mr Alberga found the upper echelons of the police hierarchy sympathetic, understanding and sincere in their hope for better relations, but, in spite of that, there were some in the ranks who had not kept faith and continued to anger the West Indian sector of the community. "The result was that West Indians doubt our ability in these representations and are losing faith in the established procedures for discussing grievances. We have taken great pains to sort the many complaints we received about the police behaviour and we select and submit the ones we find most deserving of serious consideration. In spite of this selectivity, not one complaint has ever been found justifiable by the police enquiry," Mr Alberga said.

Mr Alberga pointed out that contrary to what is often mistakenly believed, West Indians did not ask for special treatment. They only asked for equal treatment as was their right.

If there were any intentions of launching an offensive against West Indians to rid them from the country, this would ultimately prove an unproductive exercise, exacerbate ill feelings and create unwarranted tension and friction between West Indians and the rest of the country.

Response From Police Federation:

Mr Reg. F. Gale, Chairman of the Police Federation, responded briefly. He said that the Federation's platform for race relations was exemplified in the purpose and objectives for which the Conference had been convened. The Federation's concern was not only with events as they were today, but events as they will be in the future. Despite the discussions and talks which had been pursued by the Federation before with various groups at meetings and Conferences, the problems remained largely unsolved.

The greatest areas of friction and tension laid primarily between the ordinary policeman on the beat and the ordinary man on the street. It was important therefore to create some channel through which the policeman on the beat could talk with ordinary working people, so that the lines of communication for understanding and goodwill could be properly enhanced,

Mr Gale saw the need for the ordinary policeman to get to know and appreciate the backgrounds, traditions and customs of the various ethnic groups which form the immigrant population in this country. Mr Gale commended Mr Alberga for his frank, fearless and honest exposition on the present state of Police/West Indian immigrant relationships in his paper.

Mr Gale appealed to the participants to concentrate during the group discussions on the real issues inherent in this important question and to put forward useful and constructive suggestions which the Federation and the West Indian Community could pursue at the end of the Conference.

The Conference subsequently took a few question from the floor, had lunch and re-grouped into three discussion groups.

Group Discussions And Recommendations Arising From Them:

Each of the Conference group was given topics as focal points for discussions with a view to make specific recommendations. It was again emphasised that the groups should utilise the time allocated to examine the areas of conflict surrounding the particular topics in relation to Police/West Indian Immigrant relationships and make their recommendations, but it was fully appreciated that the close inter-relationship between these topics would inevitably lead to some amount of duplication of suggestions and recommendations.

Group 1 was asked to consider and make recommendations in the following areas:

> (a) Action which can be taken at grassroots level to improve relationships between the Police and West Indians and
> (b) Steps which can be taken to improve the complaints by the public against the Police; and

(Group 1, by unanimous agreement decided to include a further topic for discussion namely):

> (c) Confrontation between members of the public and the police.

Group 2 considered the following topics:

> (a) stereotyping of non-white persons by the police; and
> (b) The assumption that drug abuse is a common practice among the non-white sector of the population in Britain.

Group 2, by consensus, chose to combine both topics under a single heading for purposes of discussion and to give a balanced opinion to the main theme of the Conference viz.:

"The myths that are common among the indigenous population about the non-white sector and those held by the non-white sector about the indigenous population and in particularly how these myths have influenced the police in their behaviour towards the non-white sector."

Group 3 was asked to:

(a) Examine the system of interrogation by the Police leading up to a charge against a person suspected of committing a crime; and

(b) Examine the extent and frequency of cases of police brutality, harassment and objectionable behaviour.

The group discussions were characterised by uninhibited, serious and genuine single-ness of purpose to get down to the real issues inherent in the problem of Police-West Indian immigrant relationships and a number of recommendations emerged which the Conference agreed should be regarded as the guidelines for action to be pursued by the Police Federation and every participant both individually and/or collectively.

The following were the results of the groups deliberation:

1. Seminars and meetings on a regular basis in local areas should be encouraged and arranged between the police and West Indian immigrants to foster and enhance the dialogue. Police participation should be primarily the men on the beat, and West Indian representation should include the ordinary working people particularly, and involving the young community leaders. It was also recommended that official encouragement should be given by the Home Office on this in the form of a directive. This should strengthen the efforts which are made at local level.

2. More Police Community Relations Officers should be appointed. These officers should explore and

2. More Police Community Relations Officers should be appointed. These officers should explore and encourage face to face relationships with immigrants and work in association with youth clubs, schools, pubs and social clubs. One group also recommended that the Police Community Relations Officers should be paired with a civilian community relations officer to alleviate the fears and suspicions held by many West Indian immigrants about the police through unpleasant experiences with them.

3. Attempts must be made to recruit more black policemen. More importantly, every effort must be made to see that the current image of the policeman in Britain as an oppressive agent is restored to its former respectability to enable young West Indians to view the Police Force as an attractive career to follow. The Conference agreed that recruitment of black persons as policemen must be based absolutely on merit and not simply because it may be fashionable to have black policemen in a Police Force. The black policeman should police a racially mixed area and not be confined to a predominantly immigrant area.

4. The British policeman and police woman should be encouraged to mix much more than they do at present with the West Indian community at social gatherings. This should be reciprocated.

5. A NATIONAL WORKING COMMITTEE should be set up to follow up the work begun at this Conference to keep in touch with national development and provide background and briefing information for future seminars and Conferences.

6. Police training should be widened and intensified to include courses in human relations and background information on the social and cultural differences of

the various ethnic groups. The police should try to dispel the preconceived notion that West Indians suffer from a social deficiency and were potentially crime-inclined. A necessary part of the training of young British policemen should be placement in areas of high West Indian settlement so that they may be exposed to and become familiar with the situations in these areas before they undertake normal duties. Community relations should be a vital and necessary part of the training programme of police officers. If this were not done, lack of understanding and appreciation of the work of Police community relations officers would be nullified.

7. A nation wide "Police to People week" should be initiated by the Police during which positive attempts be made to explain the work, function and methods of the Police to the immigrant community and concomitantly members of the immigrant community and the Police should be encouraged to get to know each other as human beings. Deliberate attempts should be made by the Police to meet young members of the West Indian community to narrow the communication gap and build sound positive relationships.

8. It was recommended that for petty charges preferred against persons such as resisting arrest, assaulting the police, obstructing the police in the execution of his duty, possessing an offensive weapon, before a conviction was secured, there should be independent corroborative evidence as in the case of sexual offences. There was overwhelming evidence to show that in the Magistrates Courts, the word of the policemen was always believed, above those of the accused person.

9. The Home Office should approve panels of persons drawn from various sections of the immigrant

community, who would be able to have access to any police station to render assistance and advice to arrested persons. The panel could be designated 'HELP ON ARREST' and their names should be distributed widely to all Police Stations. Persons arrested should be allowed to name one of the panellists for consultation upon arrest. Every assistance should be given by the Police to enable the arrested West Indian person to communicate with a relative or his High Commission, or a member of the panel recommended above and his solicitor. The Conference viewed with deep concern the repeated submissions at the Conference in the group discussions of West Indian detained in custody on petty charges and brought to Court without any of the foregoing.

10. A further recommendation was that it should be made a rule of law that no person should be questioned by the police except in the presence of legal adviser, unless after a formal statement of the arrested person's rights to have a legal representative has been read to him and he signs a declaration that the statement has been read to him and he does not wish to be represented.

11. Investigation of complaints against the Police should be conducted by an independent body. In one group, the following, which received the general assent of the Conference, was passed. It reads:

"BE IT RESOLVED that with respect to complaints against the Police, Investigation Committees should be set up in various areas throughout the United Kingdom composed of officers of senior rank and independent members of the Community with representatives of coloured people and that the complainant be represented at the hearing of his complaint."

CONCLUSION:

The Chairman of the Police Federation, Mr Reg. F. Gale, responded succinctly to all recommendations which were submitted by the three groups. He remarked that many of the recommendations were already the policy of the Federation and he believed that some of the others would in the process of time become an integral part of the Federation's platform. He did not believe there was any divergence of views between those of the Federation and those of the Conference.

He stressed how much the recommendations indicated in the clearest of terms the tremendous need for improved police training and stricter supervision and he assured the Conference that the Federation would co-operate fully with everyone whose aims coincided with theirs.

Sir Laurence Lindo, Chairman of the Conference and Jamaican High Commissioner, brought the Conference to its conclusion by stating that the Caribbean High Commissioners and the Commission For Eastern Caribbean Governments would take action at the appropriate levels, and reminded the participants that the achievement of any success from this Conference depended upon everyone to take action immediately at the grassroots level of the West Indian Community and the Police.

Posterity must now look back and ask, what had changed fundamentally in Police and Black Community relationships since the above 1970 Conference was held.

Unfortunately, the situation deteriorated dramatically as a number of British cities - Bristol, Liverpool, Birmingham, London, etc. were set alight, by working class Black and White youths, at the cost of millions of

1997, over twenty five Black people died while in Police custody, without anyone been brought to book for those deaths. Volume Two of this book, 1976-1995, will discuss these issues and the response of the Black Community.

12. The Black Community And The Courts 1960-1975

The relationship between the Police and members of the Black Community in places like London: Wood Green, Dalston, Brixton, Battesea, Southall, and Bristol, Leicester, Southampton, Northampton, Notingham, Manhester, Wolverhampton, Leeds, Birmingham, Bradford and Liverpool sunk to a very low level, which erupted into Black anger, resentment, and bitterness, and poured out spontaneously on British streets. Collective anger, which was never before experienced in modern Britain, generated mostly by African people. Black community leaders, White politicians and senior police offers wondered which inner city would explode next, during the summers of 1981 and 1985. Britain's inner cities were set on fire by protesting Black youth, and joined in by White youth, who were in sympathy with their Black contemporaries.

This happened largely because the warnings were ignored by policy makers during the 1970s, when the courts were asked to deal with a number of serious charges laid by the police, against members of the Black Community. Charges which were used only in times of serious stress of a Nation. Combination of charges like riot, incitement to riot, affray, attempted murder of a police constable, grievous and actual bodily harm of police constables. These were the charges levelled by the police against the leaders of the Black Community, who stood for civil rights and liberty of all citizens. Some of these charges were also levelled at ordinary Black youth like those in the Cricklewwod 12 trial, which will be explained later.

It must be borne in mind, the record so far demonstrated that these very same young leaders and their parents,

136

were invited to come to Britain to build her economy, which they did gladly. Except for the charges placed on them, nearly all defendants so charged had never been in trouble with the police, either in the countries of their birth or in Britain. Court appearances were new experiences for the majority.

While members of the Black Community appeared in courts all over England on public order charges, the Mangrove 9 Trial was perhaps the most famous as the Police netted some of the most vocal and significant Black activists and civil rights leaders at the time. The Mangrove 9 Trial was dubbed 'a political trail' by members of the Black Community and some of the White Community.

This trial stemmed from a demonstration against police brutality at Portnal Road, Notting Hill, West London. The demonstration was necessary, the organisers believed, because members of the Black community made several complaints to the Home Office, and their members of Parliament, extending to meetings at diplomatic levels without their seeing any significant changes in the attitude of the police.

As far back as 1964, the Campaign Against Racial Discrimination (CARD) organised a demonstration against police brutality in Islington, North London Area. Again in 1967, Black people took to the streets to protest against the brutality meted out to them, this time in Moss Side Manchester. In August 1968, the BBC televised their *"CAUSE FOR CONCERN"* series, a startling account of police corruption and brutality against Britain's Black population.

In July, 1971 a large number of West Indian Youth marched on the Islington police station in North London, demanding the release of two young brothers who were unjustly arrested by the police at a funfair in the local park. The Black youth were subsequently released without charge.

On 13th January, 1971 four West Indian youth appeared in court on charges of assaulting the police and resisting arrest. All were found guilty, whose penalties ranged from fines to six months prison sentence.

On 23rd January, 1971, over one hundred Black youth picketed the New Road Police Station in Wolverhampton, in a demonstration organised by the Afro-Caribbean Circle, as a protest against police brutality in the area.

The Mangrove 9 appeared in court on 31 December, 1970. The accused were: Roddy Kentish, born in Jamaica, Rhodan Gordon, born in Grenada, Frank Critchlow, born in Trinidad, Althea Jones-Lecointe, born in Trinidad, Barbara Beese, born in England, Radford Howe (Darcus Owusu), born in Trinidad, Rupert Glasgow Boyce, born in Trinidad, Godfrey Millet and Anthony Carlisle Innis, all Black people of African origin.

The charges ranged from riot, affray, grievous bodily harm of policeman, actual bodily harm of policeman, and offensive weapon. The case ended in the Old Bailey Central Criminal Court on 16 December, 1971.
 The charges were judged in the following way:

THE MANGROVE 9 TRIAL[23]

DEFENDANT   *CHARGES*   *VERDICT*

Anthony Carlisle Innis	Riot	Not Guilty
	Affray	Not Guilty
	Grievous bodily harm of policeman	Not Guilty
	Actual bodily harm of policeman	Guilty: 9 months suspended for two years
	Offensive weapon	Not Guilty
Rothwell Kentish	Riot	Not Guilty
	Affray	Not Guilty
	Offensive weapon	Not Guilty
Rhodan Gordon	Riot	Not Guilty
	Affray	Guilty: 15 months suspended for 2 years
Frank Critchlow	Riot	Not Guilty
	Affray	Not Guilty
	Offensive weapon	Not Guilty
Rupert Glasgow Boyce	Riot	Not Guilty
	Affray	Not Guilty
	Grievous bodily harm on Police Constable	Not Guilty
	Actual bodily harm on Police Constable	Guilty: 9 months suspended for two years
	Offensive weapon	Guilty: 9 months suspended for 2 years (Concurrent)
Radford Howe	Riot	Not Guilty
	Affray	Not Guilty

Althea Jones-Lecointe	Riot	Not Guilty
	Affray	Guilty: 15 months suspended for 2 years
	Actual bodily harm on Police Constable	
	Actual bodily harm on Police Constable	Not Guilty
	Actual bodily harm on Police Constable	Guilty: 15months suspended for 2 years
	Offensive weapon	Guilty: 15 months suspended for 2 years (Concurrent) Not Guilty
Barbara Beese	Riot	Not Guilty
	Affray	Not Guilty
	Actual bodily harm	Not Guilty
	Offensive weapon	Not Guilty
Godfrey Millet	Affray	Not Guilty
	Riot	Not Guilty

As indicated in the tables above, none of the defendant was sent to prison. The 11-week trial cost the Black and White tax payers £50,000. Judge Clarke presided.

Rhodan Gordon, who sacked his lawyer and defended himself, and on whom much of the political defence of the case revolved, showed in his summing up speech that he not only had an extensive grasp of the social conditions out of which the 'Mangrove' demonstration emerged, but also a deep understanding of the system whereby radical Black protest was vilified, repressed and turned into the bogeyman of White (and Black middle-class) society. He showed, too, that the courts existed not to guarantee people their rights, but to keep them in their 'place'.

In spite of several interruptions from Judge Clarke, Rhodan Gordon concentrated upon the background to the trial and its political aspects, since he knew that it was only in getting across a measure of such knowledge to the jurors that the case would be by definition 'fair'. It was a massive task, since the very fact that the Mangrove Nine were in the box, rather than the 'heavy mod', was an indication of how far away justice was from being done.

In this he was completely successful, though the verdict only represented that in part. I reproduced here very short extracts from a four-hour speech. It was one of the most important political statements made in Britain at the time.

Rhodan Gordon said: "'Black Power mob', 'Black Power agitators'...these kind of racial remarks, the tone in which they put it over is meant to appeal to the basic fears and prejudices of White people, so that Black people can be isolated and their politics treated in the way that the prosecution here has treated them.

"The thing I resent most here - I don't care what verdict you come to, guilty or not guilty, I don't care - what I resent most of all is your bringing down Black people's politics, Black people's activity, which we're all free to carry on and do, to the level of sitting down in the Mangrove Restaurant with Mr Howe and Mr Critchlow and my good friend here, Mr Kentish, and planning to go and pelt stones at a police station, or to go and make violence on policeman. How ridiculous can you get, how low can you get ? I treat that with contempt it deserves.

"I don't know if you remember the case of [Police Constable] Challenor - he planted bricks on people, fabricated evidence, because he had a politically-motivated mind, like Inspector Stockwell, like Pc Pulley, Lewis and that lot. You only have to read their statements to know that these policemen are politically motivated. Now after the Challenor case, and things started coming to light, everybody, Black and White, had this image of the police - when they though of the police, they thought of the theoretics of the police, they didn't think of a policeman as an ordinary man, like you, like anybody else, with his weaknesses, with his prejudices, with his values, with his whole code, his attitude to life, based on his education, his background.

"I once asked Inspector Aldritt - 'Why are you a policeman ?' He said 'You want to know why I'm a policeman ? Because I hate authority and I find it the safest place to be.' I don't have an answer to that one, I just left him alone.

"Anyway - as I say, whether we go to jail or not doesn't matter. Pulley and that mod, they're probably going to end up killing someone.

"Now the police employ a public relations firm, a private firm, in contract with the police force, to brighten up their image. I don't know if that was responsible for the successful PR Press relationship they had since the demonstration, but here's something you ought to think about. For ten days running, you might have read in the newspaper an account of what happened, an account of what the demonstration was all about, and it's amazing, the distortion. You even had certain Black people coming on TV and they were party to this type of thing: 'Well, you know, this whole question of police brutality doesn't represent the feeling of the mass of Black people. I think these are isolated incidents by a couple of lunatics or something'. You had Black men coming on TV, paid by the establishment to talk that kind of stuff. So it's not just White people -Black people, too.

"And it's very interesting, the same press, like the Mirror, the News Of The World, The Evening News - they know very well that when they give a distorted account of what happens, they're giving the public an account that they cannot substantiate, and that public is the public from which eventually the juries will be picked to deal with that case. So what you have read, the impressions you may have formed a year ago of this case - that is what the newspapers whole policy was, to give the public at large a distorted picture, so that when we bring them in to the legal system to deal with them, we can guarantee a conviction. And not only get a conviction, but the sentence will be a deterrent sentence, so that Black people in Bristol or Birmingham or Islington or anywhere will say - 'Who! Boy, them getting five years, we better not do anything, it's a waste of time, because if we try to do anything we'll go to jail.' And that is what the whole scheme is about"

Rhodan gave a brief summary of the events in Marylebone Court, where the magistrates threw out the charges. Rhodan then moved on to the committal of the nine to the Old Bailey, and spoke of their decision to ask for a Black jury.

Rhodan: "We got to the point where we decided, well all right, the people who can probably best understand the kind of politics that's being played would be Black people. So we decided that to save that nasty element coming into this trial that, because of lack of evidence, people start appealing to White nationalism - meaning, appealing to you like you hear in the court up and down the country. 'The police have had their duty for year upon years upon years, they have a very difficult task of protecting us', that kind of psychology - to avoid these kinds of games being played, we'd have a Black jury. Because a Black jury could probably better understand the circumstances. I think Ian McDonald [Caucasian lawyer] was the defence man responsible for asking for that - and the judge threw it out, after two days. Could he give a reason why ? No, and that was that.

"Anyway, we decided that we'd have to put certain question to the jurors, the White jurors, to find out the type of White people who were trying our case. Because we could end up with White people who were members of the National Front. We could end up with White people who would say - 'We don't want these niggers in the country at all'. And the prosecutor gets up and appeals to his prejudices, to his fears, appeals to his insecurity, and on the basis of these emotional appeals, gets a conviction - nothing to do with the evidence whatsoever. We wanted to get White people on the jury who could understand, to a certain extent, what's really going on," said Rhodan

Towards the end of his summing up, Rhodan talked specifically about Judge Clarke's attitude to him throughout the trial, and the mystification process inherent in the judiciary system.

Rhodan continued: "The judge kept saying to me 'I am not going to stop you saying this, I'm not going to stop you saying that, I'm giving you latitude' - all this for the ears of the jury. He is saying to me, you must sit there and suffer peacefully. Well the days for that are finished and gone. I'm not going to suffer peacefully for nobody. This is 1971. If I feel an injustice is being done, I feel, like you feel, like anybody in this court feels, that it is my right, or your right, to get up and protest about it. And when I protest about it, then you can tell me why you're doing it, and I can say why I don't think it's right, and we can have a whole dialogue and come to some kind of understanding, and deal with it that way. But if you're going to use the power of the court to suppress my valid right to protest - well, that's where we come back to the whole question of violence.

"For me, mental violence is far worse than physical violence. It's all right, a slap on the face, or getting a right hander, it might burst my lip, but I can get it stitched. But to put us through the torture we've been going through here these last ten weeks - that's the most violent kind of violence," Rhodan concluded his summary.

Judge Clarke said "This trial has been a very unpleasant experience for everybody concerned...it has shown that there is evidence of racial hatred from both sides."

That was the Judge's last pronouncement of the eleven-week trial, and that seemed now to be a remarkable admission of a beaten man. The trial was a case-study in the application of radical law - its lesson could be learned in detail, but the general principle which emerged was that it was possible to fight in the courts legally and politically - and win.

It has been conventionally held that there are only two ways of approaching a trial - to get off ("the best defence money can buy") or to succumb to martyrdom ("It is far, far better thing I do...") A few radical voices in the legal wilderness at the time, always maintained that in a political trial the defendants are given little choice but to attack the politics of the bench - and that, far from proving oneself a martyr, that was the only way to win. Such a case is seldom decided on the evidence - it's more a question of who is to be master in the courtroom. If the judge is allowed to be king, then the jury will tend to be loyal subjects to his lordship's whims.

Ian McDonald (defence for Barbara Beese) hit this brilliantly in his summing-up speech:

"We've been subjected in this trial to spectacles of naked judicial tyranny. Our legal system relies on people accepting the roles they are allotted, but in this case, people have said no, we don't accept absolute power anywhere."

Often during the trial, the judge had interrupted questions from the defence. Radford Howe and Althea Jones-Lecointe, defending themselves, learned how to handle his lordship by cutting him off in midstream and suddenly firing another question at the witness while Clarke was left objecting in thin air.

Half-way through the trial, Judge Clarke, after an outrageous ruling on a piece of cross-examination by Radford Howe being irrelevant, was forced to retreat in the face of a barrage of protest from all nine defendants - "Enough of this rail-roading!" "Who's the prosecutor in this case ?" and complete uproar in court. The Black Community gained a great psychological victory when the judge adjourned an hour early and scuttled off to the safety of his chambers - the majesty of the Old Bailey had been severely dented.

The last time The Black Community played the legal game - the Oval House trial - they were all convicted of riot. The lesson of the Mangrove was - beware of lawyers, and defend yourself if you possible can. The effectiveness was based on three defendants taking the real issues of police corruption, and harassment and victimisation of Black people directly into the minds of the jury and seeking a response.

"You members of the jury are kept incommunicado during the trial. The defence at the start of the trial applied for you to be allowed to ask questions of the witnesses, but this was rejected by the judge." Ian McDonald told the jury.

The defence lawyer continued: "You are probably made nervous by the atmosphere in the court. Yet you are the only people who can take away the power of the judge, don't forget that." (Radical lawyers and would-be radical lawyers - don't forget that either).

The defence strategy, then, achieved four basic objectives:

1   It attacked the very roots of the prosecution case from every angle - legal, social, moral and political.

2   It refused to accept the tyranny of British justice at the time - the defendants always reminded the jury that a fair trial was impossible (In subsequent years a large number of alleged Irish bombers, innocent of all charges, were to bear the full brunt of injustices of the police and the courts).

3   The defence educated and embraced the jury, attempted to solicit a deep involvement from them and a real understanding of everyday racism in British society. 'The trial was an education,' said one juror afterwards.

4   The judge's traditional role of providing the decisive summing-up had been pre-empted by the defence. As one juror said: "Clarke really couldn't railroad them in that courtroom because the defendants had said so often that that's what they expected".

Before receiving a fifteen-month suspended prison sentence at the end of the trial, Rhodan Gordon told the judge: "I don't want a suspended sentence. You can give me four years, or three years instead."

The consciousness expressed in this statement from the dock was fully demonstrated the following morning - 17 December, 1971, when, on the street before his home, in broad daylight, in full view of numerous witnesses, Rhodan Gordon was "first insulted", and then "viciously attacked, prior to being arrested by PC Saunders and PC Pugh" of the Notting Hill Police Station for alleged obstruction and assault.

Though famous and a landmark in British legal history, the Mangrove Trial was not the only trial involving police and members of the Black Community and viewed at the time as political trials.

As far as members of the Black Community were concerned, their daily experiences at the hands of the police and courts were evidence of a modern civilisation repressing its Black citizens/residents.

The Brackwell Park Three[24] case was one which involved three Black youth who appeared at Camberwell Magistrates Court, in South London, on Monday, 11 June 1973. The youth were represented by Rudy Narayan. The charges were: Horace Parkinson, 19 years old - grievous bodily harm to Derek Castles, assaulting a police officer in the execution of his duty and having in a public place an offensive weapon (a car jack). Lloyd James, 18 years old - grievous bodily harm on Christopher Harper and assault on a police officer in the execution of his duty. Robin Sterling, 14 years old, unlawful wounding of Christopher Harper, assault, causing grievous bodily harm to Tucker assault, causing grievous bodily harm to Castles and possessing of an offensive weapon (a milk bottle). The youth pleaded not guilty. The youth attended a funfair at Brackwell Park, Brixton, South London, when they were arrested.

On 4 March 1974 the trial began at the Old Bailey before an all-White jury. It lasted for nine days. The defending barristers were Arnold Rosen for Horace Parkinson, Ron Rose for Lloyd James and Harry Narayan for Robin Sterling.

The line pursued by the defence was left to each barrister's discretion. The prosecution case was put effectively. Eighteen policemen gave evidence to the effect that a riot had broken out; that Lloyd James had attacked Harper and had to be forcefully restrained; that

Horace Parkinson, in going to James' assistance, had hit Castles with a car jack, and that Robin Sterling was on the wall throwing bottles, two of which wounded Castles and Tucker.

Unlike earlier trials of the *Mangrove Nine*, and the *Oval Four*, the defence was played at a low key. It took the Jury just over two hours to find the three guilty. Judge Abdela then pronounced sentences of three years each upon them. The defendants, their families and friends were shocked. That sentence brought 500 people, half of whom were Whites, on the street in Railton Road, Brixton, South London, marching against the injustice demonstrated in the case.

Another trial of twelve Black youth between 19 to 25 years old, which became known as the 'Cricklewood 12', and seen by members of the Black Community as a political trial, arose out of an incident on 12 October, 1974, in the early hours of the morning at the Carib Disco Club, in Cricklewwod, North London.[25]

The police arrived and entered the Club unexpectedly, when the entertainment was at full swing and filled with Black youth. The police arrested a young man whom they suspected to have stolen a car. Running battle between the police and the Club members ensued. Some forty two youth were detained, some of whom were charged. The police could have avoided this, by waiting and arresting the suspect, when the club finished. No one was charged with car theft.

THE CRICKLEWOOD 12 AND THE CHARGES[26]

Lloyd Ewan - Affray
Carl Watson - Affray and possession of offensive weapon
Keith Logan - Affray and possession and offensive weapon

Dennis Borell - Affray and incitement to assault police
Roy Dockery - Affray, wounding to offensive weapon
Peter Barnell - Affray and possession of offensive weapon
Joseph Smart - Affray, assault on police, and possession of offensive weapon
Neil Thomas - Affray and possession of offensive weapon
Anthony Lovindeer - Affray and possession of offensive weapon
Roger Streadwick - Affray and possession of offensive weapon
Oliver Francis - Affray and assault on police
Earl Scott - Affray and assault on police

The trial ended in the acquittals of all charges. The point being demonstrated here is the British Establishment consistently levelled these serious charges against members of the Black Community during the 1970s. Charges of affray and riot were rarely used in Britain before the arrival of Black people, and when used, only on special occasions, not in the regular and common manner as they were thrown against Black people, when they were only demanding civil rights and natural justice for all.

Barrister, Rudy Narayan, commenting at the time suggested that there was a "cross-country legal conspiracy", and he developed this theory in the following way:

" The trial of **the Cricklewood 12** is now all over. All the defendants have now been acquitted, the first nine in the first trial, Oliver Francis in the second, and Dennis Bovell and Royfield Dockery before the Court of Appeal just a few weeks ago.

and Royfield Dockery before the Court of Appeal just a few weeks ago.

"The twelve were charged following a police raid to **Cricklewood's Carib** Club in October, 1974, when both police officers and black youth were injured.

"The first trail lasted for four months, and the second trial took six weeks. The Court of Appeal judgment recently blasted the summing up of the second trial judge, Judge Abdela, for failing to put the case - based as it was on identification - properly in Law.

"Lord Justice Shaw stated in the Court of Appeal Judgement that Judge Abdela's summing up 'was the total converse of what a learned Judge should do.'

"The Court of Appeal Judgement in the **Cricklewood 12** appeal came at the same time as the results in the **Bonfire Night Trial** in Leeds, which was fought largely by Black Lawyers. At a time when there are certain Black revolutionaries' in our community who are apparently uncertain of which direction to take - these two cases are especially significant for the dynamic arrival of a group of young, aggressive, articulate Black advocates who are now notching up success after success in the criminal courts.

"The facts now speak for themselves and the critics of Black lawyers will now have to shut up. The similarity of the two cases does not end there. Both in the manner of the occurrences leading up to the arrests, to the treatment of the accused by police and the way in which both trials were fought and the number of acquittals, these two cases are much deserving of some analysis and study. To some degree they both bear striking resemblance also to the **Mangrove Nine**, the **Oval Four**, the **Metro Four,** the **Waterloo Four** and the **Stockwell Ten** trials in that police/Black confrontations in all these cases did not start off with the Blacks breaking the law, but simply with youth enjoying themselves at a dance, club, party or similar occasion. They are all therefore important cases in the very history of Black civil liberties in England.

"The **Cricklewood 12 Trial** started with police officers going into the Carib Club to 'look for a man' they alleged they had seen outside the club trying to steal a car. This is what police gave as their reason. But the club's Black Doorman, Henry Brooks, told the jurors that no such man had run into the club. In the **Leeds Bonfire Night Trial**, police said that they had had an emergency call that officers were in urgent need of assistance. But, when they got there, the officers they had gone to help said that they did not need assistance and they had not even called for it.

"In the **Cricklewood 12 Trial** it was established that prior to police entry to the Carib Club, all was 'love and peace all over the place'. It was also established that there was no trouble at all until police entered. In **the Leeds Bonfire Night Trial** it was established that prior to police going into Chapletown, there had been no trouble in Spenser Place and that people were just enjoying themselves with fireworks.

"In the **Cricklewood Trial** it was the dragging out of a man who claimed he was innocent that started the trouble. In the **Leeds Bonfire Night Trial** it was police cars driving at speed towards the crowd that started it. In both cases the majority of Defence lawyers were Black. In both cases the Defence took to the offensive and in them it was the police who ended up by being on trial. In both cases, perjury, brutality, fabrication of evidence were alleged in no uncertain terms in the ungenteel way that White lawyers defending Black people so far find impossible to achieve.

152

"In both cases the Black communities mobilised a positive response and the vibrations between Black defendants, Black lawyers and the community were total and continuos. In both cases the verdicts of acquittal handed out by the juries were without precedent in English legal history," concluded Rudy Narayan. [27]

The apparent anti-Black social engineering introduced by the police and their backers, did not lay a sound foundation for racial harmony and prosperity for the 1980s and 90s, as the future would soon to demonstrate.

13. Black-led Churches And Black Community Development 1960-1975

Black-led churches came about because Black church goers were not generally welcome in White churches. The African and African-Caribbean led Church Movement satisfied a need and led the way for independent Black-controlled institutions in Britain. Black churches, so called, were viable institutions, partly because church members were expected to give at least one tenth of their earnings to God, in this instance the Church.

Committed Muslim were expected to give 'Zkar, 2.5% and 10% for agricultural produce'. At the time, the Muslim Religion had negligible influence on members of the Caribbean Community, the majority of whom were Christians, meaning that they came from a Christian background, brought about by forced conversion during slavery in the Americas, including the Caribbean.

Black church ministers were able to buy their churches and work in a full time capacity serving their congregations. Some High Street banks were willing to give loans to Black-led churches to purchase church properties. Bank managers were aware of the congregation's financial contributions.

During the 1950s, 60s and 70s, many African-Caribbean church leaders in Britain were self-taught Christian theologians. They had no option to be anything otherwise. Britain's established church showed very little interest in the immigrants' religious affairs, even though many immigrants from the Caribbean were professed

Christians. The British and Irish missionaries taught them Christianity. Many Black church leaders went to the USA for support from the evangelical church movement. As a result, a significant number of Black-led churches were linked with the American fundamental church movement.

Black-led churches had a boom growth in all the major British cities in which Black people (those of African descent) settled.

The Shiloh United Church of Christ (Apostolic), led by Bishop Ramsey, Jamaican born, headquarters were based in East Croydon. In addition to spiritual matters, youth work and counselling services were offered, by the Shiloh. Instructions were given to new ministers, through bible courses and other religious training.

The African Methodist Episcopal Zion Church, headed by Reverend Vincent Fagan, Jamaican born, operated in Battersea, during the 1970s. AMEZC was established in the 18th century in the USA by freed Africans who were transported to America by Christians as slaves. The London Branch of this church provided youth activities, family counselling and education. AMEZC had branches in the USA, Europe, the Caribbean and Africa.

The main Church in the USA was referred to as 'Mother Zion'. AMEZC had a branch in Manchester, Shaw Temple, named after the late Bishop Shaw from the USA, who had a vision of expanding AMEZC in various parts of the world, where African peoples settled. AMEZC was different from some of the other churches frequented and managed by Black people, in that, AMEZC core leadership was African, and that was how it was intended by its founding fathers over two hundred years ago.

Other Black-led churches operated in London were The Seventh Church of Melchisedec (Spiritual Baptist) based in Harlsden, North West London, New Testament Assembly, based in South West London, Church of God, Hammersmith, West London, Pentecostal Church, based in South East London, Episcopal Evangelical Council, based in North London and the Church of the Universal Prayer Fellowship, based in South West London.

In the absence of a church building, many Black-led church members held their services in hired halls.

Ashton Gibson, Barbadian born, co-founded the Afro-West Indian United Council of Churches, as a co-ordinating body for the many Black-led churches in the United kingdom. Subsequently, The African-Caribbean Evangelical Alliance (ACEA) was formed by Black-led evangelical churches to co-ordinate the work of its many members. ACEA was led by Roland A. Nathan, an African born in the Caribbean. Both co-ordinating body were based in London, with regional representatives at various parts of England.

Reverend R. Pemberton, led the Pilgrim Wesleyan Holiness Church based in Birmingham. Other churches operated in Birmingham were the Universal Church of God, United Church of God, Church of the Cherubim and Seraphim, Church of God In Christ, Church of God Holiness, Triumphant Church of God and United Pentecostal Church of God and the First United Church of Jesus Christ. In Wolverhampton, the United Pentecostal Apostolic Church had its base. Most church organisations were registered charity. They had a common aim of service to God and man.

The growth of Black-led churches meant that branches of the more well-known denominations were established in other areas like Manchester, Northampton, Liverpool,

Bristol, Bedfordshire, Derby, Sheffield, Bradford and Huddersfield. The Jehovah Witness Kingdom Halls also attracted many ordinary members of the Black Community, particularly women. Seven Day Adventist Church Movement was another branch of the Christian religion which operated in the British Black Community.

Many of the Black ministers, though self-taught, succeeded in creating a solid moral foundation for the Black Community, particularly the children at Sunday schools. The Black-led churches were some of the true pioneers and foundation builders which gave hope to many members of the African and Caribbean people in Britain, especially those whose children had grown apart from them, or those in retirement or soon to go in retirement.

There was also a strong youth wing of the Black-led churches. Young church goers were more likely to succeed academically and less likely to get caught up in the criminal justice system for petty crimes. They were, however, still subject to the harassment by the police, partly because of racism, during the 1960s and 70s.

Black-led churches were particularly popular with the older generation of immigrants. The church offered fellowship and a sense of belonging.

There were Black ministers of the Christian Religion who were not members of the Black led-church movement; nevertheless, those ministers contributed to the Black Self-help Movement.

One of those ministers was Reverend Wilfred Wood,[28] born in Barbados and a Church of England Priest based in London.

Reverend Wilfred Wood arrived in England in 1962 and was appointed Curate and, subsequently, Priest in charge at the Anglican Parish Church in Shepherds Bush, West London.

Reverend Wood founded the International Personnel - an employment agency dedicated to finding jobs for Black people. The Agency started in 1968 in Shepherds Bush and placed 10% of applicants in jobs equal to their ability.

Reverend Wood co-founded the Shepherds Bush Social And Welfare Association. He was also co-founder of the HARAMBEE, a hostel Project based in Islington, North London, which housed homeless Black youth. He was a member of the Self-help Forum consisted of Britain's most prominent Black activists at the time, who were pioneering major projects in the Black Community, which subsequently had lasting impact on Black and White Britain. Members of the Forum were George Campbell, Leader, South East London Parents Organisation; Oscar Abrams, Leader, Keskidee Arts Centre; Herman Edwards, Leader, Harambee Project and Vince Hines, Leader, Dashiki Council. Reverend Wood was subsequently appointed the Bishop of Croydon.

The Rastafarian Movement, as a religion, had important influences on the Black young people at the time, particularly those who came from the Caribbean and experienced 'culture shock' and rejection by the 'host' community. The Rasta Movement provided a strong foundation of cultural entertainment, particularly the reggae music which originated in Jamaica.

Some of the Rasta groups which existed at the time included The Ethiopian World Federation, set up by His Imperial Highness Hail Selasie, late Emperor of Ethiopia. The British Branch was called local 33. The Rastafarian Universal Zion Group, The 12th Tribe, The Rastafarian Women's Organisation and International World Federation. These groups provided nursery activities and information and advice on matters dealing with Rasta. Work was also done with Black prisoners, who were of the Rastafarian Faith, dealing with of diet and dress code.

The Muslim Faith had very little influence on Black immigrants from the Caribbean, during the 1950s, 60s, 70s and 80s. That situation was to have dramatic reversal during the late 1980s, with the arrival in Britain of African refugees, who were practising Muslims in Africa, and the success of the USA based Nation of Islam among Black youth in Britain.

Many members of the Black Community set up their own Freemason Lodges. Some immigrants, from places like Jamaica, where there was a tradition of Freemasonry, carried on their practices in England. By the nature of the Freemasonry, being a secret society, members were reluctant to discuss their membership and activities. Many people, however, joined this type of secret organisation for social and professional reasons. A belief that fellow Masons would help in times of need.

14.   Black Business And Credit Unions 1960-1975

The history of Black Business Development in the United Kingdom (UK) represents a microcosm of the issues affecting Black people in Britain, particularly those of African descents. Racism was institutionalised in Britain during the 1950s, 60s and 70s.

The high street banks were not the sort of institutions that would consider lending capital to people of African descents, in order to set up businesses. People of Indian descent were fortunate to get some loans from the banks, who got their business ideas off the ground.

The first generation of Caribbean immigrants who arrived in the UK did not plan to settle. Most gave themselves five years to work sufficient money and return to their home lands and improve their quality of life. They did not take into account macro-economic interplay. There were no fiscal concessions for the Caribbean immigrants, nor were wages sufficiently high to create an escape route from rising costs and other dynamics of an industrial society, with an eroding economic base, fighting off the efficiencies of their competitors.

The 'transient' labourers from the Caribbean were here to stay and now relegated by racism to 'third class' citizens, who provided the backbone of the Public Transport Sector, the National Health Service and the large industrial plants.

Britain operated a mixed economy and it was inevitable that members of the immigrant communities with courage and determination would identify commercial opportunities and exercise the necessary entrepreneurial skills to maximise those opportunities. African and

Caribbean entrepreneurs established businesses to provide entertainment facilities, Caribbean foodstuffs, beauty aid and other specialist goods and services for the readymade but limited market of the African and Caribbean immigrants, now saw themselves as permanent residents, with special needs.

In Liverpool during 1951 George Wilkie, born in Guyana, managed the local Caribbean entertainment club - Collsy House, which was successful as a local business. Herbie Higgins, a West Indian who served in Britain's armed forces during World War II , remembered it well. Herbie said: "There were demobilised West Indian servicemen after the war. They wanted a place to enjoy themselves and we went to George's Club. There was another Club in the area, called the Colonial Club - Stanly House. That was run by the English"

In Pread Street, Near Paddington, London, during the mid 1960s and late 1970s, another successful business, the "Q" Club, and later called the "People's Club", a night club, which was managed by Neville Campbell (Count Suckle), Jamaican born. The "Q" Club was a popular entertainment venue, frequented by the famous and the unknown. This initiative started not from a bank loan but by self-help.

The Rio Night Club, based at Westbourn Grove, Notting Hill, London, was managed by Frank Critchlow, born in Trinidad. The Rio operated between 1959-1969, at which both immigrants and native English men and women attended, for good social entertainment.

In Manchester, during 1956, Aubrey Lee Lawford, born in Jamaica, started in business on his bicycle selling cakes. The business grew, and later called the 'Pioneer Bakery'. It was based at 55 Hogne Road in Old Trafford. That was one of the first Black businesses in

Manchester. Most of the Caribbean immigrants were working on the buses and in the factories.

A mixtures of ex-servicemen and newly arrived immigrants and members of the White community who supported the Pioneer Bakery. Ten years on the Pioneer Bakery had a fleet of vans - twenty or more, transporting its products to places like Bristol, Cardiff, Luton and Watford. Aubrey Lee Lawford retired and his business was closed. Another bakery initiative in the area also enjoyed success, which was owned by Bill Read, born in Jamaica. These initiatives were the exception, operated by people who would be successful in any system.

Aubrey Lee Lawford first worked as a Joiner and, in the early days, operated his business during the weekends. He made 'bulla cakes', initially, and sold two together to his friends and colleagues at work during their break time in the local factories. This type of business initiative did not require a loan from the bank. Later Aubrey and his wife Rebecca were able to open a grocery shop and Off Licence - a shop which was licensed by the authorities to sell wines and spirits.

The above initiatives were the type of business ventures, which Su Su, Partners or Throwing Hand, helped to finance. These were forms of part lending/part saving money schemes. This self-help 'thrift' was used to great effect by the people both in Africa - the 'Yoruba Tribe', and the Caribbean, when they did not always find the Saving Banks welcoming. Initial capital for this venture came from pooled wages, later called community credit unions.

This type of self-financing worked when a number of people would join together and each put up a specific sum of money called 'hand', each week, corresponding to the number of persons involved. From week one, and the following weeks, each member would receive his/her 'draw', which amounted to the total collected, which could be any amount from £50 to £1000. This was dependent on the number of people involved and the amount each was required to contribute weekly. For example - if ten people were involved and each was expected to contribute £10 weekly to the pool, each of the ten would get (£10x10) £100 when it was their turn to collect.

The Collection was called the 'pool'. That went on until the cycle came to an end, when all contributors had an opportunity to collect. The cycle restarted in reverse order. One of the great advantages with the scheme was that, apart from accumulating a large sum of money in a relatively short space of time, one could also get last and first draw, doubling the amount. The entire scheme ran by a member of the group - 'the banker'.

This system could only work if members had a regular income to put in the pool. This type of financing was not adequate to develop consistent entrepreneurial structures with large capital outlay, and that type of 'venture' money was not made available by the financial institutions, to members of the African and Caribbean Community.

By 1975, the business side of that Black Community remained under developed, as greater emphasis was placed on social welfare matters, including the growing race relations industry. Most young professional Black people went into the social welfare sector rather than in commerce and industry, partly because of the lack of significant venture capital.

Some example of the type of Black businesses in 1975 were: West Indian World Newspaper, S.H. Weathers Plumbing Services, St. Clair's, specialists in hairs and beauty treatment, Claud Brooks Caribbean Entertainment Agency, Gems Model and Entertainment

Agency, Human Hair Wigs And Hair Pieces Club, Hairdressing Academy, Calabash, L.E. Campbell's Westindian Travel Agent, Starlight Travel Service, Freighting And Shipping Agency, Rainbow Travel, Mavis Marshall Beauty Clinic And School, Phillip Lewis Homeopathic Centre, Dyke And Dryden Hair Products, Coach And Horses Public House, Rio Night Club, the Mangrove Restaurant, Back-A-Yard Restaurant, Spathodia Development Co. Ltd., Real Estate Agency, Dougie's Hideaway Night Club, The Bouncing Ball Club, Spiritual Card And Palm Readers, etc.

As an attempt to enter business, over 28,900 [1]people, most of whom were West Indians, of African origins, were recruited between 1969-74 into a Pyramid selling scheme called Holiday Magic (Great Britain) Limited.

It was reported during the 1970s that the West Indian Community lost £33 million pounds to Holiday Magic, with which Sir Julian Hodge, Caucasian, and his Finance Company were associated. This scheme involved the buying and selling of cosmetics - get rich quick scheme. Many described it as a 'swindle.'

The 'Holiday Magic' episode had devastating consequences on many - 26 people reported to have committed suicide, 214 committed to mental institutions, having heard that they lost their life savings on Sir Julian Pyramid Scheme.

The Holiday Magic victims were assisted by the Birmingham based Mutual Protection Association Against The Effects of Pyramid Selling, supported by the Westindian Federation Association. James Hunt, born in Barbados, was the leading light in both

---

[1] Stephen Bulgin, West Indian World Issue No 296. 25/31 March, 1977 - PYRAMID: Allegations Refuted, page3. Published by Lenmond Publishing Ltd., London.

organisations. Ten and three quarter million pounds (£10.75m) were recovered from Sir Julian's Finance Company and paid over to West Indians who lost their money.

West Indian immigrants were easy prey for all sorts of swindle. They believed what people told them, partly because the West Indians judged people by their own very high moral standards and integrity. The West Indian would not 'con' anyone, and so no one would 'con' them. Very simplistic reasoning; but that might have helped them to survive the overt racism they faced daily in Britain at the time partly because they did not understand it.

This type of experience put off a large number of potential Black investors in business ventures, who were unlikely to take business risks again.

The African and Caribbean Community in Britain needed a specific national co-ordinating and promoting body. In 1974, William Campbell, Jamaican born, assisted by Sammy Jay-Holder, Grenadian born, Len Renwick, Trinidadian born and Robert Govender, Jamaican born, undertook a series of public consultations, via the media and public meetings. A 'Caribbean Chamber of Commerce' was formed in 1976, as a 'complementary' body, instead of a National Black Business Development Body, which the organisers believed would form 'sometime in the future'.

15.   The Notting Hill Carnival - An Initiative Of The British African-Caribbean Grassroots

THE NOTTING HILL CARNIVAL was created to soothe the social pains, heal the Spirit and retain hope in the minds of the Black people in Notting Hill during the 1960s and 70s.

It was an escape for a people who were struggling with the core inequalities of eurocentric urban civilisation, and its own brand of the Rule Of Law. The Carnival was an overt declaration - a metaphor, by its creators, which said that the immigrant community had something to offer to Britain. Take it or leave it.

To the White working class, the Black working class said - 'the Carnival is good medicine', tried and tested in the British colonies. A medicine which provided comfort and merriment to the ordinary people, who stood up and maintained their dignity in face of repressive colonial rule from London.

History's irony brought together the children of the colonials and the descendants of the African forefathers to the heart of the ex-Slave Owners' and Colonials' Citadel - London, England.

Notting Hill is a District in West London, in the Royal Borough of Kensington And Chelsea, a very rich Borough of London, which was administered by the Conservative Party during the 1970s.

The people who settled in Notting Hill during the 1950s, 60s and 70s, came mostly from Trinidad and Tobago, Dominica, Guyana, Grenada, and a sprinkling from

Jamaica. The area in Notting Hill at which the poor - Black And White - lived was off Westbourn Park Road, Westbourn Grove, St Stephens Gardens and Powis Square touching on Ledbury Road.

The Socialist broad sheet *'The Red Mole',*[1] said of *Notting Hill in 1971: "Notting Hill, a ghetto harbouring the oppressed - hippies, the unemployed, unmarried mothers, Irish, those who have fallen foul of bourgeois 'law and order' and of course, black people. It is a self-aware Community".*

There had been a significant Jewish population in the area during the 1940s and 50s, and they built their 'Tabernacle', as evidence of their presence, which became disused as the Jewish population moved out to affluent districts.

Notting Hill Gate was a cosmopolitan area. It had significant slums owned by slum landlords, one of whom was the late Perec (Peter) Rachman, born a Polish Jew in 1920, who was said to have escaped from one of Adolf Hitler's concentration camps in 1940, and ended up in a labour camp in Siberia until 1942. Rachman arrived in England in 1946, and after a year in re-settlement camps he went to work in a factory in the East End of London. He moved to Bayswater, near Notting Hill Gate, in the 1950s and entered the property business and began to acquire local properties.

Many of Rachman's tenants were West Indian immigrants during the 1950s and early 1960s. Peter Rachman died in 1962 in London, and his name became synonymous with slum and bad landlords.

---

[1] The Red Mole - 'Smash Racism'. Published by Relgocrest for 'The Red Mole', 182 Pentonville Road, London 1971

The Encyclopaedic World Dictionary defined "Rachmanism" as 'a system of extortionate landlordism involving overcrowding of slum properties, esp. with coloured people, exploitation of racial prejudice and other pressures to drive out existing tenants, and, finally summary eviction before renovating the property and letting it at higher rents.[2] This definition gives an idea of the sort of social pressures the Black people of Notting Hill were experiencing. That situation arose because of the failure of the British Government, which invited the West Indians to Britain, and did not make adequate housing provisions for them, and so they were driven in the hands of Rachman type landlords.

Black people were subjected to racial harassment on the streets by White youth called 'Teddy-Boys', during 1951-1960, and the West Indian Community lost Kelsor Cochrane, a carpenter, 'murdered by the Teddy-Boys' in 1958, which caused one of Britain's significant post war street riots by people of African descents. The attack on Cochrane was recorded by members of the community as a race attack, and that added notoriety to Notting Hill. That also showed that the ordinary members of the White Community were not prepared by the authorities to accept the influx of Black people from foreign lands.

West Indians were happy and gay people, easy going, with a deep love for life. They liked the good things of life, like music and creative arts. They were particularly expressive in the way they communicate with others. They were prepared to adopt to any reasonable proposition. The West Indian, those of African descent, mixed well. They liked *their* loud music as an expressive form of communications. The Italian, Latinos people were also known for their overt expressiveness. That was opposite to the Anglo-Saxon's English reserved.

---

[2] Definition by Encyclopaedic World Dictionary, Hamlyn Publishing Group, London 1971

Loud music was therefore a part of the West Indian culture. They came from an open society, and lived most of their lives outdoors, and those who were at home, would have their doors opened. The tropical heat would demand nothing less. In Notting Hill, some White neighbours complained to the police and the local authorities about the West Indians loud music.

The immigrants brought with them their way of life. Mr Winston Churchill who invited the West Indians to Britain, on behalf of the British Nation, knew of the West Indian way of life, before the invitation was issued. No one should be surprised, therefore, to hear loud music coming from West Indian residence.

The average West Indian household would have bought some of the best brands of radio and gramophone equipment on the market, some of which were 'Grundig', 'Blue Spot' and 'Telefunken'. These guaranteed good, clear and loud music, with a heavy bass line, with almost stereophonic quality. Hi-fi/stereo type of sound came later. West Indians could afford to buy these consumer products because they saved among themselves through community credit unions, which was know as 'Su Su', 'Partner' or 'Throwing Hand', in effect part lending/part saving money schemes.

The West Indian immigrants in Notting Hill would have played imported music, like - calypso, ska, bluebeat, jazz, rocksteady, Black American rock 'n' roll and blues. Reggae and soul were to come later. The West Indians were not used to spending most of their leisure time indoors, and they continued to play their music, because that was all they had as any real entertainment, which they could call their own. They had to adjust to the British climate.

White neighbours, the few who did, continued to complain to the authorities, and the police made their visits and asked that the music be turned down or off, and tension built up. The White complainants called the West Indian music 'jungle music'. The West Indians did not have ready access to social clubs in London because of 'colour bar'. The usual racist signs were clearly displayed: 'No coloured. No Irish. No Dogs'. Exceptions were the 'Roaring Twenties' and 'The Flamingo' in the West End Of London, which offered membership to some West Indians - mostly students, forces personnel and visiting tourists, who would normally be entertained by Jazz and soul music.

The 'Q' Club, based at Pread Street, North West London, was managed by Jamaican born Bill Campbell (Count Suckle), provided a mixture of Black music, during the mid 1960, but the venue was not large enough to accommodate significant numbers, and membership fee was expensive. The Club catered largely for USA enlisted men on weekend pass and the up-ward mobile African and Caribbean people and their guests.

The Rio Night Club, 1959-1969, in Notting Hill would offer 'black' music, with the latest from across the Atlantic - Jamaica, Trinidad and the USA. Space was not adequate at the Rio to satisfy the entertainment needs of the growing number of West Indian immigrants locally.

It was necessary for those West Indians living in the English ghettos to create their own entertainment. They did. They held house parties, and if a basement was available, they would hold shebeens - private social functions, with music, drinks and food, which went on into the early hours of the mornings. (The sort of hours, similar to the time which the very rich would leave their private and exclusive clubs in the West End of London).

Some house party organisers charged a small entrance fee to pay for electricity and pocket money for the people who were providing the Sound System - (mobile disco music), and recuperate their expenses through asking their 'guests' to make contributions for food and drinks. The police alleged from time to time that shebeens were sometimes used to peddle marijuana and alcohol. Many of those social functions were raided regularly by the police, looking for any drugs and alcohol sold on the premises illegally.

The people who attended such parties were West Indian workers who were working in the factories for long hours, at lower wages than their White colleagues. Others would have been nurses, midwives, doctors, bus drivers, bus conductors and students. They faced racism daily and they were five thousand miles away from home, in the Caribbean. Later, the people who came directly from Africa joined other Africans from the Caribbean, in experiencing racism in Britain.

By the middle of 1960s, many West Indian parents sent for their children who were left in the West Indies. Fiancée sent for their love ones and married. Things began to change as more and more West Indian teenagers arrived to join families. The young were less tolerant than their parents, of racial insults, in schools, on the streets and at the work place.

They had pride in their blackness and culture - their music and creative art, and were not prepared to have them put down by people who had not understood, or attempted to understand, the richness of the African and Caribbean culture among them in Britain. Black youth embraced the slogan *'I'm Black And I'm Proud'* and *'I'm Black And Beautiful'*. Terms which were hardly used by Black people who lived in the British colonies in the Caribbean for over three hundred years.

This stand got the Black youth in difficulties with their parents, who took the line, initially, to suffer quietly. As a consequence of their stand, many Black youth became homeless and on the streets and the police was on their case, as it were. Many found themselves in remand homes, borstals and prisons.

By 1972, the sum total of most West Indian residents in Notting Hill was: slum housing, exploitation and racism at the work place, and in schools (West Indian children were wrongly placed in educational sub-normal (ESN) schools), restrictions on their way of life, police attention, racist attacks on the streets and homelessness among Black youth.

In spite of that type of unpleasantness, the West Indian immigrants were able to build up friendly relationships with many ordinary White people, particularly the male, with female members of the Irish Community.

The Notting Hill Social Council, The Notting Hill Housing Services, with George Clark, Caucasian, and the Peoples Association, a collective of multi-cultural membership, gave vent to some of the social pressures which were being experienced by the West Indians. These organisations made genuine attempts to help, with better housing, play-groups and participation in the Claimants' Union.

Roony Laslett, a Caucasian community worker, was supportive to members of the African Caribbean Community in the local area. This support included good information and advice and representation about current social conditions to the powers that be. Andrea Shervington, Guyanese born, was one of the leading lights of the Notting Hill Peoples Associations. The Neighbourhood Law Centre, with backing of the Law Society, and legal aid support, was introduced in Notting

Hill in 1969, with Peter Kandler, the Senior Solicitor, and a member of the Jewish Community.

The Dashiki Council, headed by Vince Hines, operated a youth hostel/community education centre in Notting Hill for homeless Black youth in 1971. The CAC Training Workshop Project, founded by Rudy Kentish, Jamaican born, operated in Notting Hill also in 1971. The Workshop, based on self-help, was set up to train unskilled youth of the Notting Hill area. The Black Intermediate Technology, directed by Louise Chase, born in Barbados, was introduced as another Black self-help initiative to assist unskilled Black youth in Notting Hill where the needs were particularly pronounced. These Black self-help initiatives operated with the goodwill of public donations, and skilled volunteers from the Black Community.

For local children four years to eleven, the Malcolm X Montessori Programme was established in April, 1970 to provide summer activities. These activities were offered to both Black and White children who were on summer break from mainstream school. The Programme's basic foundation was that 'children should not be encouraged to compete with one another in any field nor should they be encouraged to be self centred egoist - necessity of co-operation in life must be stimulated with logic...each child should be kindly and carefully handed.'

It was against this background that Trinidadian born Lesley Palmer (called by some - Teacher Palmer) rejuvenated the yearly Trinidad type Carnival on the streets of Notting Hill in 1970. The idea and initial organisation of the Notting Hill Carnival was attributed to Trinidadians who lived in Notting Hill. The very early Carnival started in 1965, with a few people walking the streets playing their music instruments. However, the Carnival did not gather significant momentum until the early 1970s.

Members of the local Black residents needed an outlet. They needed to be given back their creative spirit. They needed mass. They needed to 'jump up, jump up' and express themselves in rhythmic ways as they, as Africans, knew best. They needed to escape racism, at least for a little while.

The Mangrove Restaurant, along all Saints Road, owned by Trinidad born Frank Critchlow, was an important base for the meeting of the Notting Hill Carnival Committee and supporters. The Mangrove was like a miniature community centre, which came out of The Rio, which was also managed by Frank Critchlow, situated at Westbourn Park Road, Notting Hill, during 1959-1969. The Back-A-Yard Restaurant, at Portobello Road, owned by Grenadian born, Rhodan Gordon, in the same area, was also a place sometimes used to discuss plans for carnival activities.

Other members of African origins who were frontline organisers of the Notting Hill Carnival were: Sylvyn Baptise, Victor Critchlow, Bigger Hamilton, Merle Major, Frank Critchlow, Darcus Howe, Althea Jones (later to be known as Althea Lecointe), Edmond (Eddie) Lecointe, Basil Javis, all born in Trinidad. Other members associated with the 1970s Notting Hill Carnival were Barbara Bees, English born of African And Caucasian parentage and Rhodan Gordon. [1]

Black youth from the local Metro Youth Club, which was set up by the Local Authority Padding Youth Committee in 1968, and based at St Luke's Road, supported the development of the Carnival, some of whom were Jeb

---

[1] There had been many more people who worked as a team to make the Carnival a success. However, this work is not a study of the Notting Hill Carnival, but its birth and early years, and the social, economic and political factors which contributed to that pregnancy, during 1965-75, and the social relief the Carnival brought about.

Johnson, Cuthbert Pierre, both Dominican Born, Alfie James, Jamaican Born and Errol Pascal ('Blues'), Trinidad born.

The core planners of the Carnival were born in Trinidad, who often referred to the development of the Carnival as, 'a we ting', meaning, the Carnival is ours. Participants brought their own music and costumes. No grant money was sought and none given. The initial concept of the founding fathers and mothers of the Carnival was based on self-help. The organisers knew that grant givers, giving to initiative like the Carnival, had a way of engineering the conditions for the initiative to be taken over by people of their choice, and that was not always within the interest of the ordinary people, for whom the Carnival was created.

The early Carnival attracted only a few people. By 1975, ten years after the carnival idea was first floated, it began to attract thousands of people from all parts of London and the provinces. It also attracted the police, and it was not long before the inevitable confrontation occurred, between the police and the young people at the carnival festivities, which inflicted serious embarrassment on the Police, on national and international television. Large groups of police were shown to be on the run, chased by angry young Black citizens.

The people who put the Carnival on a higher profile were Black Conscious activists, and the Carnival was a direct result of the Black Conscious Movement of the mid 1960s and 70s. The Leadership of the Movement was determined that members of the local Black Community would not be defeated by racism in its covert and or overt forms, particularly racist attacks on the core culture of the African and Caribbean communities.

Yet, the Black Conscious Movement recognised, and made adequate allowances in the philosophy of the Carnival, to accommodate the qualities of the ordinary members of the White Community, who wanted to enjoy Black people's art forms. All were welcome in peace and good-will. That Spirit remained with the Notting Hill Carnival.

While members of the Black Community experienced greater social hardships living with Rachmanism, it was also recognised that within the local slums were ordinary members of the White Community, who borne no malice or ill intent to their Black neighbours. This civilised approached was universally welcome by members of the Black Community.

By 1975, serious tension began to show among members of the police force and Carnival goers. There was an over-kill of police in uniform sent to police the Carnival, to the extent that it would seem that there were more police at the Carnival than civilians. That was dubbed by members of the Black Community 'the police carnival'.

It was, of course, *not* a police carnival, and that brought more resentment among members of the Black Community, particularly among Black youth, who saw the police high profile as an intrusion in the only substantive entertainment event that Black people could call their own.

The Carnival focussed positive attention on Notting Hill. Slum houses were torn down and others refurbished by the Westminster City Council and the Royal Borough of Kensington And Chelsea. The relatively new Notting Hill Housing Trust (NHHT), a registered charity, founded by The Reverend Bruce Kenrick, Caucasian, was supported by the Housing Corporation, a government agency. NHHT received public donations to purchase slum houses, convert them into flats for families and rent them out at affordable rent, under the provisions of the 1965 Rent Act.

The Act laid down the duties and obligations of landlords and tenants. John Coward, Caucasian, was Director of the Notting Hill Housing Trust in the early years, and contributed significantly in laying the foundation for the Trust's success in the years to come, providing social housing for many thousands of multi-cultural people in South and West London. Pansy Jeffreys, an African born in Guyana, and Lionel Morrison, of Zulu ancestry, born in South Africa, must also be given credit for their contributions to the Notting Hill Housing Trust at Committee level. Out of the Notting Hill slums came a number of important social pearls, initiated by members of both the Black and White Communities, which had lasting values.

We saw that the Notting Hill Carnival came out of a people who had to live under serious social pressures and threats of racism daily. As a result of taking a positive stand, by using culture as a basis for change, the poor and dispossessed created a monument to, and one which had important influence on, Britain's wider culture. Benefits which extended even to those with profit motives in the wealthy White suburb. Black people and their Carnival brought substantive trade and civic pride to the Notting Hill area.

The Notting Hill Carnival was to become the pride and joy of Britain and the largest street festival in Europe, sometimes attracting one million people to its two-day events over the August bank holiday weekends - Sunday and Monday.

Today, Notting Hill type of carnivals is being organised annually by ordinary members of the community all over Britain's inner cities, including Birmingham, Bristol,

Leeds, Luton, and attended by Africans, Caribbean, Indians, Filipinos, Japanese, Pakistani, Bangladeshi, Arabs, Jews, Chinese, Caucasians, and others.

The down trodden have power when they are united in diversity and embrace natural justice.

The Notting Hill Carnival Initiative was *Black self-help* at its very best, during the 1960s and 70s. That Spirit of resilience and creativity is still with the Community today, ready to be embraced by those who are in need.

16.   The Birth Of Britain's Black Self-Help Social And Welfare Movement 1965-75

In 1968 the conflicts between some West Indian parents and their newly arrived children were matters for concern. Youngsters up-rooted from the Caribbean and brought to join their parents, whom they might not have seen for five to ten years, brought with it elements of resentment. The children underwent a 'culture shock', which was their inability or unwillingness to assimilate, at their exposure to Britain's social environment. An environment which many considered to be hostile to them.

The children had no counselling to prepare them for England. In addition, those who were of school age, had to adjust rapidly to English school life. Some have had to take eurocentric intelligence tests (IQ), the questions and symbols of which were culturally bias, unfamiliar to them, which resulted in many being classified wrongly as 'educationally sub-normal'.

Those young people who were too old for school had the added task of finding a job or an apprenticeship of some sort. They would have been expected to register at the Labour Exchange (subsequently called the Employment Exchange). Many did not have the required qualifications to be offered apprenticeship or the skills to get jobs with careers prospects.

Many ended up going to the factories and doing the same jobs which their parents were doing, where there were plenty of vacancies. In any event, they would be expected to live at home with their parents. They would be unlikely to find accommodation partly because of a genuine shortage of available housing and colour bar.

Most West Indians are Africans, and Africans are normally strict in bringing up their children, particularly on the question of having respect for the elder and authority. The youth would be expected to be back indoors at a time stipulated by their parents/guardians, which were not always agreed by the youngsters and that added to tensions at home.

Invariably, the break came, particularly with the male, which resulted in their leaving home, without their giving serious consideration to the magnitude of their decision. By leaving home meant that they became homeless and at risk.

The risk they were likely to face could not be imagined by West Indian born children, since there was no comparable social situation in the society from which they immigrated.

Those children who remained in school invariably complained to their parents of some teachers and pupils negative attitudes towards them. Parents were unlikely to believe their children, particularly on matters dealing with complaints against teachers. West Indian parents believed that English teachers were part of an extended family, as it was in the Caribbean, where teachers looked after their pupils in a family atmosphere, in the absence of their parents. On the strength of that belief, many West Indian parents did not consider the importance of attending regularly parent/ teacher meetings, except when there were crises involving their children. No one told West Indian parents initially that there was a significant difference between teachers attitudes in England and those in the Caribbean.

That same West Indian attitude was applied to the relationships between their teenage children and the police. When children complained to their parents about police malpractice towards them, the parents did not believe, and often seriously reprimanded them for 'spreading malicious information about the police'. West Indian police would not harass an innocent person and so it followed that the English police would not do that either. West Indian parents did not learn about racism and colour prejudice.

However, they eventually learnt about prejudice, under the broad heading of 'colour bar', the term used during the 1950s, and 60s. That lesson was quickly assimilated when West Indian parents could not explain any longer the attitude of some white skin residents towards them. Many joined or support Black pressure groups, like the Caribbean Education And Community Workers Association (CECWA), the North London West Indian Association, The Black Parents' Movement (BPM) and the South East London Parents' Organisation. In these matters, London normally took the lead and the provinces followed after issues were clearly defined on relevant matters, affecting members of the Black Community, like setting up supplementary Saturday Schools and hostels for homeless Black youth.

Unfortunately, the youngsters collective experience at home, having the people they trusted most rejected their concerns about teachers and police racial prejudices, added more tensions between parents and children.

The immediate impact on most Black teenagers was that they were unable to get jobs or accommodation suitable for their requirements. The majority were not prepare to do the menial jobs offered to their parents. They wanted appointments which would lead to 'proper training' for their future. That attitude was seen by some parents as that their youngsters did not want to get a job to earn and help with some of the household bills. If that situation continued, it would also lead to the youngsters leaving home.

Some of the consequences for girls leaving home often resulted in their starting a family prematurely. It was especially difficult for a single unmarried female with children to find accommodation - Black or White. Britain was still being influenced by the legacy of Victorian moral values. Yet many Black female youth believed that if they were pregnant they would be made priority for housing by their local borough council housing department.

The average person on the street still referred to children born out of wedlock as 'bastard'. The signs exhibited by landlords, shop-keepers and others, spoke for themselves: "No children". "No coloureds". "No Irish". "No Dogs". When the Race Relations Act of 1965 and 1968 came into being, overt racism went underground. Racism became covert, but equally potent.

British Social Services were not geared to cope with West Indian parents and children home conflicts. That was a new area for social workers, who were normally from White middle class backgrounds. Social work training did not, in substance, take into consideration Britain's multi-cultural society. Often parents and youngsters kept home difficulties away from the social services, partly because they did not know who they were and what they were. Moreover, which child wanted to 'bring shame on the family', as it would have been viewed at the time, in taking home matters to strangers. Nevertheless, some West Indian families did seek social services help, which resulted in their children removed from the family home and placed in local authority care, via the courts.

Recognising the potential social crisis of the West Indian Community and what that situation could lead to in the long run, the Racial Adjustment Action Society (RAAS) was formed in 1968 by Michael Abdul Malik (also known as Michael Defretas and Michael X), who was born in Trinidad, of a Caucasian mother and African father.

Michael X was the first person to be sent to prison for twelve months under the British new Race Relations Laws of 1968-69, for a speech he made to West Indian nurses in Reading, Berkshire. Since that sentence, no other person has ever been convicted and sent to prison under those Laws by the courts, up until the present day. The conviction and length of sentence created a sensation in the infant Race Relations Movement, at the time, which lost the significant confidence of members of the Black Community. The argument was that 'the very laws which were brought in to protect members of the Black Community seemed to have been turned against them' That case brought national notoriety to Michael X.

RAAS set up *The Black House Project*, based at 95-101 Holloway Road, Islington, North London. The purpose of the Project was to provide emergency housing for families and single homeless young people, with an emphasis on West Indian families and young people, who seemed to have been experiencing a higher proportion of homelessness.

Michael X, President of RASS, who preferred to be known as 'Chief Servant', explained:[29]
> "The Black House is a Centre where people come to. It is a Power House, which does a number of different things. It caters for a people who have always associated with degradation and squalor, a situation which epitomised plenty for people in general throughout the country. It is

a place of study, where people are able to study things like our history and languages. It is a Centre which has created the very first Black Library in the country and has the most extensive books by Black writers. It is a place where the very first black museum in the White western world was created and has the first collection of black arts outside of the British Museum. It is a place where people had poured their life blood into removing bricks, which was fallen and broken into an ambience of life. It is a place where a church has been created, which has created a guidance, to be had to those who need it. People eat and drink inside the Black House. There is a workshop and a laboratory for studying situations that no other laboratory can study in this country.

"The main philosophy which we teach in the House daily is that we can and should serve each other, and we do that.

"From the Black House we can institute certain programs like our repatriation program. One must think in terms of a wilderness for example, or a priory, when the White man went into America there was a vast expansive open priory, where the Indians lived and the White man created an enclave, which he called his fortress, and from there he was able to culture the end result of what he owned in the country - the entire country. It is necessary for us to have institutions which can look after the welfare of our people. Whether our welfare is one which will be lasting relationship with other races, whatever it is - we are suppose to create institutions which can take care of business, and this particular institution is one which has been created just like that," Michael X concluded.

The conversion of the Black House property would cost £250,000. Although the work was not completed, the building was used as a community centre for young people, who had nowhere to go during the days. It housed three homeless families and a number of single men. Twelve bedrooms were available. When the conversion was completed, the building would house a restaurant, a mini-supermarket, cultural centre with lecture room, a library with books written by Black writers, a rarity to find such books at the time in the public libraries or the stationers - a small museum and a small mosque and residential quarters.

The Islington Council refused planning permission for the conversion to go ahead and the White neighbours complained about the loud music coming from the Black House, during youth club evenings. The Council placed an order on RAAS to "stop playing and producing music within two days", which was issued on 28th August, 1970. The reason for refusal was that "such things were incompatible to the surroundings".

Brother Herman Edwards, born in St Lucia, the Caribbean, and Secretary to RAAS, analysed the situation as it was on 20th May, 1970:[30]

> "We are concern with the situation of ourselves - Blacks in a White world. The brotherhood of man is important, but since we Blacks stand in an unequal situation, for us the brotherhood of the Black man is a priority. Each of us must therefore take the responsibility of seeing that his own house is in order, and then take a stand for his own self-respect and manhood.
>
> "Economically and politically this placed us at the bottom of society. To do something about it is our responsibility because those who have power will

185

always fight to keep it. We are aware that ex-Colonialist Powers who for centuries have ruthlessly exploited our territories are here geographically in Europe. We are in Europe today in large numbers. It is our sworn duty to serve all of our people by any means necessary whether they be in South America, Africa to the Caribbean.

"The Black Power Movement in England made Brother Michael their Chief Servant. He in conjunction with other brothers, decided that as a primary stage we should launch out on a program to benefit especially the young brothers and sisters, that is, to build a community centre, The Black House. We therefore acquired a number of buildings on Holloway Road, North London, for this purpose, which today is described by many as an urban village. We let many people as possible to know about our Project. Naturally this created resentment in the Establishment who do not wish us to have any semblance of power, money, property, influence or communications.

"I, as Secretary, feel that it is my sincere duty to inform those who are interested in the brotherhood of the Black man, and not in the behaviourists of the White secretarian society, therefore, appeal to you for help.

"Further to the above, I may state it is not our aim to antagonise our neighbours. We wish to be left alone to live in peace and love with the world at large. Our motto is non-violence. But our views are strong," Herman concluded.

The Islington Council's decision was a devastating blow to the Project and its homeless families and young people, and the Council was not offering to house the

Black House current residents. RAAS closed the Black House initiative in light of the Islington Council's decision. The needs which RAAS identified was still there, only more intensify, which history would soon to demonstrate ten years later.

The Black House was the Pioneer to Black Self-Help in social and welfare work in Britain. The difference was that the Black House combined a number of objectives under one roof, including housing, which other initiatives at the time did not achieve.

There were community centres in places like Manchester and Preston specifically built by West Indians as social and recreational facilities, like the Preston West Indian Centre, the West Indian Centre and the West Indian Sports and Social Centre, in Manchester and the Merseyside Caribbean Council, in Liverpool, opened in 1974. Similar facilities, in Tiger Bay, Cardiff, Wales, were managed by Africans, like the Sons of Africa Organisation, some of whose members were British born Africans, descendants of African merchant seamen. The common link associated with these groups was that they provided services to their members and friends, who would not get such culturally sensitive services elsewhere.

Manchester had some of the most committed Black activists. Berry Edwards, born in Guyana, and Warden of the West Indian Centre, had been in the front of standing up against racism, from the early 1960s throughout the 1970s, one of Britain's most repressive periods against her Black population.

Another example of Black people's solidarity in 1975 was clearly demonstrated by Aston Douglas, Aubrey Lee Lawford, Aston M. Core, Joseph M. Dolton and Joseph A. Dias, who pooled part of their wages and, those with houses, re-mortgaged them, in order that the local West Indian Community could have a centre of their own. That was not a private enterprise venture. They became trustees of the Centre - not directors, and, as individuals, did not benefit in any financial way.

All of these men were born in Jamaica and came to Britain during the mid 1950s. They were bus drivers, joiners, and factory workers. The purpose built Centre housed the West Indian Sports And Cultural Club, in Moss Side, Manchester.

While the Black Community in Bristol did not own a centre of their own, the West Indian Parents And Friends Association, under the Leadership of Jamaican born Owen Henry, the West Indian Development Council, under the leadership of Paul Stephenson, Bristol born, of African parentage, Pioneer Club, under the leadership of Jamaican born, Prince Brown, all provided social and welfare activities for their members. Paul Stephenson and his Council gained national attention during the 1960s for the stance taken against the local Omnibus Company and its management policy of alleged racial discrimination against members of the Black Community in travel and employment.

During the late 1970s the Black population - in Birmingham, Woverhapton, Leicester, Northampton, Swindon, Derby, Sheffield, Southampton, Bolton, Leeds, Coventry, Bradford, Ipswich, etc began to establish culturally sensitive community social facilities, as a direct result of the initiative being taken by members of the African and Caribbean Community in London. With the advent of black-owned news print in Britain during the 1950s onwards, Black people living in the regions were able to be better informed and network with other immigrant settlements elsewhere in Britain.

The Newly constructed motorways, like the M1 laid in the early 1960s, facilitated easier travel for everyone and made it possible for regular visits to relatives and friends at various parts of the country, particularly in the industrialised areas where most of the immigrants settled.

Black people had been living in Scotland for over 200 years, many married local Scottish natives and faded away with little trace. However, more recently during the Second World War, Africans from the Caribbean were assisting the Forestry Commission in Scotland, helping the war efforts.

By 1968, one Scottish hospital, Bridge Hern, had between 30-40% staff of African nurses from the Caribbean. Edinburgh University was famous for training African students from Africa and her Diaspora, in the Caribbean, many of whom returned to their countries of origin on qualifying, after their staying between two to three years. The majority of Black students resided on the university compus during their time of studies, and so they had no need to search for accommodation or jobs in the wider society, as such, there was no way to test the levels of racial discrimination in Scottish society.

Since 1923, the Edinburgh University West Indian Students' Union looked after the welfare of Black students. In the mid-1960s the Union changed its name to the 'Edinburgh West Indian Student's Union', which opened the way for membership to those nurses who were not attending the university. By 1982, the name was again changed to the Lothian Caribbean Association, chaired by Barbadian born, Eman Hope.

The Association purpose was to further the welfare of Caribbean people by virtue of a multi-cultural program. More Chinese and Indians lived in Scotland relative to people of African origins .

Given this history, Scotland did not experience the social impact of having significant settlers from the Caribbean, as was the case in England and Wales. It would seem that there was no need for the Scottish authorities, therefore, to establish special facilities for Black people, during 1945 and 1975.

In 1969 the Council For Afro-Asian Peoples (CAAP), under the Presidency of Jamaican born Vince Hines, mindful of the social situation among members of the Black Community, resolved that one of CAAP's aims - *"to provide where necessary nurseries, playfields and homes for our children and to provide youth clubs for our ever increasing number of youth."* - should be implemented at the earliest.

A research was undertaken, headed by Vince Hines, the result of which brought into being the Dashiki Council, which focused on housing and educating of homeless Black youth.

This was after two years working with a group of Black youth in the Ladbroke Grove area of Kensington and Chelsea, West London, the Holloway Road area of Islington, North London, the Harrow Road area of the City of Westminster, West London the Lisson Grove area of the City of Westminster, North West London, and the Edgware Road area of North Paddington, North West London, between 1969 and 71.

Many of the homeless youth with whom the Dashiki organisers came in touch were some of the most militant, whose views were shaped by their experiences, some of whom had ' harrowing stories to tell of confrontations with the police and their dogs, on the streets, at social gatherings, alleged drugs plantings and other humiliating experiences at the hands of the police.'

Dashiki, therefore, began its work with the youth. The first Council of Trustees was made up of George Lamming, British resident and the celebrated Barbadian writer, Pansy Jeffry, born in Guyana, Community Worker, based at the Labroke Grove Citizens Advice Bureau, Reverend Wilfred Wood, born in Barbados, Church of England Black Priest, Philip Kossoff, Lawyer, member of the British Jewish Community, Victor Burnett, born in Guyana, Accountant and Vince Hines, Writer/Journalist/Broadcaster. Mike Philips, born in Guyana, Teachers/writer, Buchi Emacheta, born in Nigeria, Writer, and Donald Kinch, born in Barbados, Teacher/writer, were appointed Education Officers subsequently. The Council was registered with the Charity Commission. There was a separate Executive Committee for the operational management of the Project's activities.

Details of Dashiki's work, contained in its first annual report dated 1972/73, are reproduced below:

"The Dashiki Council Annual Report[31]

1. INTRODUCTION
   (a) History
   After an intensive research three years ago into the social background of second generation immigrants it was discovered that a large number of black youngsters were without homes. It was estimated at the time that in London alone as much as a thousand of these youngsters between the ages of 15 and 21 years were of no fixed abode.

   The youth were generally without skills, the majority came to join their parents at 6-12 years old. They came into conflict with their parents who, to the youngsters,

191

were 'strangers' who accepted the values of their social environment which the youth rejected, because they believed that such social values were refusing them proper housing, education and jobs. Communications broke down between parents and youngsters, which resulted in the youth leaving home on the 'drift'. Later it was also discovered that an increasing number of immigrant children born in Britain were having similar problems to those who arrived in Britain at an early age.

The added conflict between cultures is also a contributory factor to the social situation of the youngsters. They are undergoing certain internal crisis as they search sometimes, fruitlessly for their identity and manhood, not knowing who they are, what they are, and where they are going. The situation is of such concern that the Home Secretary asked the Community Relations Commission to look into the question of unemployment and homelessness among ethnic minorities in Britain and report on the policy implications of the findings.[1]

The 1971 census showed that 16.2% of black youth were without jobs. Without a home and a job, many of these youth ended up sitting aimlessly during the days at amusement centres and bookie shops; at nights in all night cafés, restaurants

[1] The Rt. Honourable Robert Carr, MP, Home Secretary. 'Unemployment And Homelessness: A Report'. Published by the Community Relations Council. ISBN 0 11 340563 4, 1974.

and night clubs. In the small hours of the mornings, at the end of it all, the youngsters dispersed in the following ways:

i.   Some are 'lucky' and find space to sleep on friends' floors

ii.   Some get arrested and sent to remand centres

iii.   Some head for bus, railway and tube stations, derelict houses and open parks (in the summer), snatching as much sleep as possible on the moving transport or on the park benches, poised to carry on the cycle.

iv.   Some just move about, perhaps finding drugs to keep them awake

Inevitably, the majority of these youth got into trouble with the police which often resulted in their being sent to penal institutions.

The organiser, Vince Hines, converted his large flat at 59 Lisson Grove, London NW1, into a community for youngsters in chronic need. These youngsters were referred to the Project by the Probation Service, Local Authority Social Services, Voluntary Organisations and individual self referrals. It was out of this experience that Dashiki (defined here as Shelter and Protection) came. Subsequently, the Dashiki Council was registered as a Charitable Trust.

The Organiser recognised from the beginning that it was not enough to provide just a bed for these disadvantaged youngster - more than that was needed.

(a) Aims

Therefore, if the Dashiki Community is to be genuinely useful to the people with whom it deals, it must be based on a self-help concept, providing the following services:

i. Temporary accommodation
ii. Supplementary tuition and advice on how to follow further education
iii. Legal advice on relevant matters
iv. Information about their welfare rights
v. Advice and help to secure suitable employment, training from government centres and similar training schemes in the private sector
vi. Help and advice as to how to secure second stage and permanent accommodation
vii. Pastoral care and counselling towards self-sufficiently.

These services are alternative to a small extent to the facilities the youngsters did not have the opportunity to have in society.

(b) Need to Expand

Because of the pressures on Dashiki to expand, the Notting Hill Housing Trust

(NHHT) was approached for a suitable house to lease. A house was found and the NHHT offered Dashiki a five-year lease on the premises at 139, Ledbury Road, London W11. In addition, the NHHT agreed to do the conversion of the house at a cost of £4,500 to be paid by Dashiki over a period of five years.

The agreement was finalised by Dashiki and the NHHT. By August 1972 conversion and decoration of the premises were sufficiently advanced so as to make the premises operational to have an intake of homeless youth.

Six staff were engaged and the second Dashiki Community came to life.

Dashiki grew to be a national example as an alternative to providing disadvantaged people a communal way of life. The serious newspapers in Fleet Street carry favourable publicity on the Dashiki Project. People from different parts of the country came to visit Dashiki, who invited members to visit and advise them as to how to set up similar Dashiki Projects in their areas.

2. NEW PREMESES

   (a) The Lebbury Road Community caters for administration, recreation and residential quarters. More space is still needed.

   (b) The Community

The residential unit at the Community can house comfortably twelve youngsters at any one time. Because of the pressing needs for more similar accommodation it is important that Dashiki expand its residential units. Dashiki has a waiting list of over 40 youngsters, which stretches longer daily. This number is enough to fill another four communities. For a family atmosphere, the ideal number in any one residential unit is 10-12 youngsters. Beyond that number, the atmosphere becomes impersonal, which detracts from the warmth of a communal way of living, which is necessary to help to correct the youngsters feelings of rejection.

(c) The Community as a Stabilising Factor:

The Dashiki Community is used to help to stabilise those youngsters who are still at home and visit the Community. They participate in similar supportive, therapeutic and advisory facilities as residents'. Adding to the number of residents, another 600 youngsters visited the Community since it was opened.

Dashiki would like to respond to greater demands, but, because of limited facilities the Project is unable to do so.

(d) Dashiki Supplementary Education Programme:

The Dashiki Community also offers supplementary education programmes to young residents and associates, which take in current affairs, social studies, careers guidance, ethnic studies, welfare rights, legal rights, group discussions and personal tuition in general education. Volunteer lecturers visit the community and assist with these programmes. The youngsters respond to the programme surprisingly well.

(e) Visits to Courts, Borstals and Prisons:

The Dashiki Welfare Team members see as part of their responsibility, the visiting of, and writing to, youngsters in penal institutions. Because of the social situation of the youngsters on the streets, court sessions become a common place. This part of Dashiki work is time consuming, but valuable. Volunteers play an important part in this side of the Dashiki operations.

(f) Abuse of Facilities:

Anxieties are sometimes caused by the minority of those youngsters who sometimes abused the use of the facilities at the Community. This is understandable. It is not easy for youngsters of such varied backgrounds to live within a community, where one is expected to share with others the facilities available. This demands a very high standard of self-discipline and self-respect. This is very much a part of the training of self-reliance being instilled in the youngsters in order to help them face the outside world with some confidence.

(g) Residents:

Period of stay at the Dashiki Community:
Residents are placed in three main categories:
i)   Emergency: youngsters who need a bed for only a day or two after which

they return home and sort things out with their parents

ii) Temporary: others might only need shelter for a week or two

iii) Part-permanent: on the other hand, there are those who need a longer stay to sort themselves out which might last for up six months or more. The general need, however, is support on a part-permanent basis, sometimes caused by the general job and housing shortages.

Dashiki makes efforts to bring youngsters and parents together. But it is often found that many youngsters objected strongly to returning home to live. In situations of this nature, Dashiki does not force the issue.

3. STAFF:

(a) Great demands on staff:

Because Dashiki is to some extent seen as an experimental project, great demands are placed on the staff on matters as speaking engagements, agency visits, home visits and so on. To cope with such pressures, Dashiki adopts a system of specialisation. A worker specialises in careers guidance and education; one in social and welfare; another in fund raising and publicity and so on. Dashiki now has six staff. Because of pressures of work and the continued need to expand, more staff are needed to work with the youngsters.

(b) Student Placements:

Talks have been held with various colleges of further education about their student placement at Dashiki. So far the Project has had such a placement from the Goldsmith College, Whitelands and North Western Polytechnic are equally interested in this scheme.

(c) Volunteers:

As mentioned, volunteers are assisting Dashiki in its Supplementary Education Programme, visiting and writing letters to youngsters in penal institutions. Volunteers also helped in the decorating and painting of the Community [House].

(c) Trainee:

It is the general policy of the Dashiki Project to train as many suitable youngsters interested in youth and community work. The Project has put that policy into operation, and on its staff there is a full-time trainee youth and community worker selected from ex-residents. There is now a general and serious shortage of youth and community workers of the youngsters peer group.

4. DASHIKI RELATIONSHIPS WITH OTHER ORGANISATIONS:

(a) Statutory

i)   Probation Service:
       Dashiki has been in contact with the Probation Service ever since its birth. In fact, the Probation Service Youth Resettlement

Project at Borough High Street in one of Dashiki's chief contacts in sending homeless youngsters to the community. Local probation officers also keep in touch with the Project, in their difficult search to place their Black youngsters.

ii) Prisons, Borstals and Remand Centres
Dashiki maintains certain contacts with penal institutions at Aylesbury Prison, Huntercombe, Portland, Dover and Holensy Bay, borstals. Many youngsters within these institutions leave for London without a home to go to, which obviously means that they are at risk and generally end up returning to a penal institution from which they came.

iii) Local Authority Social Services:
Many of these youngsters (15-18) are under some form of care order [by the courts]. Some have been offered placements in traditional hostel type of accommodation, which they refused. The youngsters seem to want accommodation of a supportive nature. As a result, local authority social services are some of Dashiki's chief referral agents. They too seem to have special difficulties in finding accommodation for Black youngsters.

vi)   The Police:
        Dashiki keeps in contact with the
        local police Community Liaison
        Officer

iv)   Social Security:
        Dashiki has a good relationship
        with the central and local officers
        of the Department of Health And
        Social Security (DHSS). This
        department shows certain
        progressive imagination in helping
        to alleviate the problems of
        homelessness among the youth.
        There is room for continued
        progression.

v)   Employment Exchange:
        Dashiki also has a good
        relationship with the local
        employment exchange. The Inner
        London Education Authority (ILEA)
        careers local offices have also
        been co-operative. Special
        assistance has been given to
        Dashiki by the Martin Luther King
        Foundation Employment
        Exchange. They have been
        particularly active in helping
        Dashiki placing youngsters in
        suitable employment.

vi)   Hospitals:

        The Tavistock Clinic (Adolescent
        Unit) have been working with
        Dashiki. Dr Perin's, [Psychiatrist],
        advice and assistance have been
        most helpful.

vii)   The Community Relations Commission:

The CRC has been working closely with Dashiki and has given practical assistance to the Project.

(b) Voluntary:

It is Dashiki's policy to work closely as possible with other voluntary bodies. Dashiki is in contact with the following groups: - The Harambee Project, in Handsworth Birmingham and Islington North London. The George Jackson Trust in Manchester, Prince Brown House in Bristol, SHELTER, The National Association For The Care And Rehabilitation of Offenders (NACRO), Soho Project, Centre Point, RELEASE, Black People's Information Centre (BIPC) at 301 Portobello Road, London W10 which has been most helpful and the Ladbroke Grove Citizens Advice Bureau.

(c) Youth Clubs:

Dashiki also keeps in touch with the following clubs at which many of the homeless youngsters frequented: Metro Youth Club,[based in Labroke Grove, London Borough of Kensington And Chelsea], Cryptic One Club,[based in North Paddington, London Borough of Kensington And Chelsea] 70s Coffee Bar,[based in Harrow Road, City of Westminster], Big Five Club, [based in Harrow Road, City of

Westminster]Gresham Project[based in Grasham Road, London Borough of Lambeth] and Keskidee Centre[based in Gifford Street, London Borough of Islington]

5.   THE FUTURE:

As mentioned, there is a need for Dashiki to continue to expand. From the present stretching waiting list of youth needing a place to live, along with other forms of support, it is clear that the services Dashiki offers are in great demand. The project has now come to be known as giving identification, hope and leadership to the youngsters with whom it deals.

6. DASHIKI IMMEDIATE NEEDS:

a) Financial assistance to purchase long-life properties
b) Financial assistance for the appropriate conversion of such properties
c) Financial assistance for the employment of staff to run such premises
d) Financial assistance for the off-setting of administrative costs incurred in   the running of the Dashiki Council.

7. CONCLUSION:

The Dashiki Council has demonstrated its ability and willingness to face the challenge with certain measure of success in face of its limited resources. The continued growth of an organisation such as Dashiki depends partly on the goodwill of other people with adequate resources to share.

203

Dashiki thanks all those people who have generously assisted it financially, morally and otherwise, over the past twelve months, and looks forward to their continued assistance in the future.

It goes without saying, however, that the alleviation of the social pressures of people should be the concern of all reasonable people. Others would put it down to the responsibility of the State. That might be so; but until the Sate decides to make that total move, there are some of us who believe that we should do something positive now. With this knowledge, it should not be necessary for Dashiki to make any 'special' effort to attract the sort of necessary assistance it requires to carry on its necessary work.

Dashiki maintains: 'Give us the resources and we shall teach the youngsters to help themselves'.

Board of Trustees March, 1973 "[1]

The Dashiki was funded by public donations and private and statutory grants. By 1975, a serious dispute in style of management and development of the Dashiki Programme occurred among members of a newly elected committee, which caused a fatal schism. Dashiki was subsequently re-organised, called the Vince Hines Foundation, and re-launched as a National Charity, in 1975, which focused on education, training and community development matters.

New trustees were brought on board. These were: Venis Buckle, Prince Brown, Frank Cousins, Vince Hines - all were born in Jamaica; Donald Kinch, Louise Chase,

---

[1] Annual Report filed with the Charity Commissioners, London, 1973.

Gilmour Smith - all were born in Barbados; Lionel Morrison, born in South Africa, of Zulu ancestry and John Lloyd, born in England, and a member of the Jewish Community. Except for John Lloyd, the trustees were of African origins, specialist in their individual field.

The Dashiki House was closed in 1975. However, from the important pioneering work of Dashiki, grew a significant and strong movement of self-help initiatives in Britain and abroad, which dealt with social and welfare matters, including community education and training. Some of the initiatives which were modelled on the Dashiki example were: The Youth Foundation, Leicester, with Tyrone Zampalados, born in Antique and George Thomas, born in Jamaica; Pioneer House, Bristol, with Prince Brown, born in Jamaica; The George Jackson House, Manchester, with Ron Philips, born in Guyana; Melting Pot Foundation, Brixton, London, with Ashton Gibson, born in Barbados, Rene Webb, born in Jamaica, Owen Sylvester, born in Jamaica, Creg Noel, born in Barbados and Alfred Dubs, born in Nigeria.

Other similar initiatives were: the Harambees - 1 and 2 in London, with Herman Edwards, born in Antigua, and Brother Sam, an African born in the Caribbean; Harambee in Birmingham, with Jack David, born in Jamaica; Harambee in Leeds, with Byril Harriot, born in Jamaica and Rupert Morris (Pastor Morris) Hostel, in North London, with Rupert Morris, born in Jamaica. Attached to each of these residential type projects were small education and advice units, as the Dashiki plan envisaged.

Short term funding for these initiatives were provided by central government in partnership with local authorities, under urban regeneration programmes, the Community Relations Commission (CRC), under a broad heading of 'self-help' funding, 1971-85 ('Self-Help Funding' came from aid money which should have been given to Idi

Amin's Uganda, and withdrew by the British Government, as a result of the matter associated with the Ugandan Government expulsion of Ugandan Asians). Other funds for Britain's Dashiki type programme came from private trusts and foundations, although Black-managed groups funding from this source was less pronounced. The major part of funding came from services on offer by the projects.

An Housing Corporation was created in the early 1970s by the Government to develop housing associations and co-operatives, and provide affordable rented homes for people with housing needs, working with the National Federation of Housing Associations, many of which operated under the Industrial And Provident Society Act of Parliament. The 1966 Local Government Act , section 11, was designed to give disadvantaged citizens access to funding for special needs, including 'all those born in another country of the Commonwealth however long they have been resident in the UK, and their descendants.'

There were Black pioneers in youth clubs. Sybil Phoenix, born in Guyana, founded and operated the Pagnell Street Youth Club, based in the London Borough of Lewisham, during the late 1960s and 1970s. This Initiative was one of the first Black youth clubs to operate in London, which had brought hope for many of its members. The Famous Shaka Sound System came out of the Pagnell Street Youth Club. (A 'Sound System' is a mobile disco unit, which had been the primary source of entertainment of Black youth during the 1960, 70s and 80s, operated from youth clubs and hired municipal town halls, and at private premises, at a time when members of the Black Community were hard pressed to find adequate entertainment venues of high standards. See Chapter seventeen of this book, *'Maintaining Cultural Identity In Face Of Racial Hostilities 1950-1975').*

There were pioneers in giving information and advice to members of the Black Community. Many members of the immigrant community used the local citizen advice bureaux, if they knew about them. During the 1970s there was a growth of law centres, normally staffed by a qualified solicitor who applied for legal aid for any client they took on board. These had been useful to members of the Black Community. The North Kensington Law Centre, situated at Golbourne Road, West London, was well used by the local youth in Ladbroke Grove. Peter Kandler, a member of the Jewish Community, headed that Centre. While the above provided good services to those who visited them, they were not Black self-help initiatives.

'ADVICE',[32] an Immigrant Advice Centre, was founded in June, 1970 by Louise Nwaogu, born in Nigeria, and Rene Webb, Jamaican born, under the auspices of the Community Development Trust. This Centre was one of the first that was set-up and ran by members of the Black Community and gave services to a multi-cultural clientele.

ADVICE aimed to educate immigrants as to their legal rights and to mediate between the Black communities and the Establishment.

Louise Nwaogu, ADVICE Director, preferred to be called Brother Louis, who said: "We are a free 24 hour service, and since we were formed two months ago we handled two hundred and eighty cases. Most of our cases come from Brixton, Notting Hill Gate and Islington.

"Immigration problems are also typical of those cases with which we have been dealing. People at airports not knowing what to do call us for advice. People within the country waiting for deportation find our advice useful," said Louise Nwaogu.

ADVICE had a Panel of Black and White lawyers, doctors, social workers and students. Members on the Panel were volunteers, eighty per cent of whom were African, West Indian, Indian, Pakistani and Malaysian.

It was the organisers' view that the Black Community had serious problems, and those problems must be solved essentially by Black people, 'we are realistic to realise that White people with just minds have a vital part to play in applying that solution.' ADVICE , a charitable concern, was financed by other charitable bodies and located 283 Gray's Inn Road, West Central London.

St Johns Inter-racial Club was an early pioneer in offering a mixture of information and advice. One of the leading lights was Courtney Laws,[33]who was born in Jamaica.

In 1958 the St. John Inter-racial Club was founded in Brixton, South London. The Club members recognised the racial discrimination that was prevalent and decide not to wait on the wider public to offer the things they needed to make their stay in England more comfortable and ease some of the social stresses.

There was no suitable place of entertainment for the people arriving from the Caribbean and most of those who came were relatively young. The Club started to organise programmes for social activities, including dominoes, visits and house parties. Members moved around the community to meet others. The idea was to get to know as many people possible. In doing that each could give help where it was needed. The Club was self-financing and it organised outings for its members and their friends.

By 1970, St John Inter-racial Club moved to be called The Brixton Neighbourhood Community Association

(BNCA). Immigrants who came relatively young were getting relatively old and a different type of service was needed. Some people were thinking of returning to the Caribbean, others were uncertain as to what to expect were they to return. Some were ill and could not return home, and the background to all this was racism. The new services on offer in 1970 were advice and counselling, sheltered and social club for senior citizens, school education, welfare, drugs advisory unit, small business development and holiday projects.

Courtney Laws emphasised that Black young people should understand as a matter of duty what their elder had to suffer in England to build organisations so that the young would not go through the same hardships as the older ones did - their fathers, mothers and grand parents.

"Black people must now seek to own things, and make sure that these things will never be taken away as happened in the past," said Courtney Laws.
He continued: "Finally, I would like to say to the Black Community that irrespective of the difficulties that confront us in society today, irrespective of the stress and frustrations that we have got to put up with, let us become and remain strong and determined, so as to prepare a very deep-rooted and concerted effort towards our progress and development, based on our created Self-Help concept for the future of our children and Community."

BNCA became Brixton's largest Black-managed Community based organisation supporting a number of centres. It is partly funded by grants and donations, but it covers a substantive part of its running cost by the services it provided to members of the community. As Chairperson of BNCA, Lionel Morrison, born in South Africa, also played an important role in the development of the Association in the early years. In the front line of supporting and developing BNCA was Wilhel (Rubie) Laws, born in Jamaica.

The Black People Information Centre (BPIC) was formed by Rhodan Gordon, Grenadian born, and Tony Mohipp, Trinidadian born, in 1971. Rhodan Gordon was involved in the historic Mangrove 9 Trial [1] at the Old Bailey which ended in December of the same year. BPIC was based in Portobello Road, West London, and self-financing. By 1975, Cecil Gutzmore, born in Jamaica, joined BPIC.

The BPIC was situated in the heart of the social revolution that was taking place during the 1970s in Britain, and throughout this period BPIC ensured it provided professional advice to beneficiaries usually self-referrals.

In housing, the BPIC campaigned against racism, harassment, evictions and bad housing. The single homeless was of special interest, as so many Black youth were homeless at the time.

In addition, BPIC provided a specialist reference library of books, mostly written by Black writers from the Caribbean, USA, Europe and Africa. Writers whose works were not yet available in public libraries. This service on offer was specially important to Saturday supplementary school organisers who needed books on Black history in order to give Black pupils and students that necessary sense of purpose, identity, self-esteem, pride in themselves being a member of a Black Nation with over 250,000 years of history behind it.

The Black Self-Help Movement and the literacy associated with it sought to stem the tide of *cultural genocide* - that is, when one culture seeks to impose

---

[1] See reference notes 23 'Mangrove Nine Court Report'

the repressed culture losing identity, direction, purpose and traditional self-disciple, and forced, therefore, to imitate the aggressor's culture. At the end of the day, those who are being repressed begin to experience depression, mental illness, suicidal tendencies, substance abuse, family tensions and break ups, lawlessness, self-hate and the lack of confidence in self. The sort of things being experienced by members of the Black Community in Britain, particularly among young African and Caribbean male. Great Britain is making them mad.

Beneficiaries were, therefore, at ease in a centre of BPIC's type. They were assured of an objective and yet sympathetic ear. Service offered was culturally sensitive - the tone and style readily understood, and a follow up of each case was assured.

BPIC engaged in campaigning. That came about during the 1970, when there appeared to be a culture of police malpractice. That is, as soon as one case was resolved, the same person returned for the same type of support, basically a continuos conflict with police and the local Black youth.

On health issues, members of the immigrant community were relatively healthy and least likely to overuse the National Health Service. There had been no specific health concern, which needed community health initiatives by members of the Black Community during the 1950s, 60s and early 70s, except Sickle Sell Anaemia, and Thalassaemia, which were hereditary blood diseases which affected mostly people of African and Asian origins respectively.

Neville Clare, sickle cell suffer, born in Jamaica, was a pioneer of Sickle Cell Research in Britain. He founded the Organisation for Sickle Cell Anaemia Research (OSCAR) in 1975. Through his initiative, many thousands of people in Britain, came to know about sickle cell anaemia and thalassaemia. A suitable climate was created so that sickle and thalassaemia suffers could be diagnosed and treated with understanding.

Volume Two of this book will discuss the period from 1976 to 1995.

17. Maintaining Cultural Identity In Face Of Racial Hostilities 1950-1975

A People without an understanding of Self is a People unable to define its past, present and future. A People without direction is a People vulnerable at the mercy of predators, exploiters, wickedness, injustices and inequalities, groping in the dark.

During the four hundred years of Colonialism and the period of Slavery sometimes referred as the Plantocracy many millions of African mostiy from West Africa, were shipped to the Western Hemishere[1]

The most prominent forms of African musical expression were banned, under threat of death. The drum was subverted, the playing of it was seen as a challenge to the authority of the Planter Assembly. The dances and rhythms that emanate from those tradition were suspended. The resilience of the African however was apparent in that some of these practices in musical, and artistic expression were kept alive, although in time these became synthesised with European customs such as Quadrille, one of the familiar dances brought to the Caribbean by slave owners.

After emancipation in the early nineteenth century, the Identity of the African was debased. The re-emergence of the drum began with esoteric cults. These movement gained respectability rather late in the day. Parang in Trinidad and Guyana, Pocomania and Rastafarian

---

[1] Wolde Selassie, 'The Caribbean Experience In Art', published in Self-Help News, Issue No.7, London, 1986.

drumming chants in Jamaica, were some of the accepted forms of this evolution.

Shango, Legba and Belle were also evident but less well known. The changes that were known, brought about by the declaration of independence, and the radical Pan-Africanism Movement, associated with several innovations, like Calypso, (Soca - came later), Ska, Bluebeat, Rocksteady to Reggae music.

That was part of the cultural background of the people from the Caribbean who immigrated to Britain between 1945 and 1970. By 1962, the 'rush' of immigrants from the West Indies declined. Those from the Sub-Continent of India brought with them a culture and tradition over five thousand years old. Those From the Continent of Africa, brought a tradition which was as old as Humanity itself. The Africans from Africa and the African Diaspora, had a special difference, they were converted in mass to Christianity, which was the slave owners' and colonials' religion. Some Africans were Muslim, but not a significant number settled in Britain between 1945 and 1975.

The Asian position on religion was settled. They were mostly Hindus, Buddhists, Muslims, and Sikhs. That was a very important start in Britain. They knew that they had to establish their own places of worship in their new home. That was not the perception of those immigrants coming from the Caribbean and parts of Africa. As far as they were concerned, they were coming to a 'Christian' Country.

The people from the Caribbean and parts of Africa had expectations. They took for granted that they would have integrated into the already established English religious communities - the Anglicans, Catholics, Baptists, Methodists and other Christian denominations. The newcomers were surprised when they were not welcome warmly in these religious institutions on their arrival.

The resilient spirit of the African people came into play, and they formed suitable religious institutions for spiritual fulfilment, in order to maintain their collective identity, as far as was possible in Britain.

Not all immigrants wanted to go to church or the mosque. Black people introduced the Sound System - loud amplification of music, mobile disco, super gramophonic Public Address System (PA) - in order to satisfied their entertainment needs. Public Address System had always been in Europe, in the town halls and at large public functions. This System was adopted by members of the Black Community in England to provide culturally sensitive entertainment for a large number of people.

The first Sound System was introduced in London during the mid 1950s, by Vincent Forbes, born in Jamaica. The System was called *Duke Vin.* Vincent Forbes had his base in Ladbroke Grove, Notting Hill, later to give birth to Europe's largest street party, the Notting Hall Carnival. Duke Vin Sound System was inspired by the Jamaican based Sound, *Tom, the Great Sebastian,* during the 1940s.

England was like 'a grave yard' during the 1950s and 60s. Radio stations were off the air by midnight and, except for the very rich at their exclusive clubs in the West End of London, nights were quiet. The workers were encouraged to go to bed early to get up on time for work in the factories, the offices, the docks, or where they were employed in the mornings. Most English live music was the ballroom type. Cinemas were still big business, as Television was in its infancy. Live music was the order of the day, which spurned many big bands. So many that the population could listen to brace bands in some parks at purpose built band stands. The Salvation Army brace bands could be heard playing on the streets - 'onward Christian soldiers'.

Rock 'n' Roll was on the horizon. If members of the White working glass wanted to hear it, they would have to tune into medium wave and listen to *Radio Luxembourg,* an unofficial radio station based in Luxembourg, Europe. While some immigrants from the Caribbean listened to some 'rock 'n' roll' from time to time, calypso, ska, soul, gospel, jazz, blue beat and rock steady and later reggae were preferred.

Live Black jazz bands from the USA were imported by Caucasian promoters. Bands like Duke Elington, King Curtis and the likes. Members of the immigrant communities hardly attended these functions. Jazz lovers might go to the Flamingo, Ronnie Scots, later the 100 Club in Oxford Street, The Roaring Twenties Club, the Lyceum in the West End of London. Rhythm and blues were also the 'in' music for White middle class Britain during the 1950s, 60s and early 70s.

That was not enough to satisfy the entertainment thirst of an immigrant population who were largely factory workers, bus drivers and conductors, doctors, nurses, midwives, hospital orderlies, cleaners, students, servicemen and women. Black diplomats had a wider choice of entertainment venues. Even then, they too were subjected to racism.

There was, therefore, a need for the Black Sound System, and it grew and provided an important service for members of the African and Caribbean Community. Some of the popular names of 'sounds' during the late 1950s, 60s, and 70s were - Duke Vin, Count Suckle, Count Ken, Lord David, Lord Delly, Neville King, Duke Read, Count Shelly, Sir Wisard Sound Machine, Sir Coxsone - 'The Creation Dub Rocker', Jah Shaka, Black

Patch, Fat Man Hi-Fi, Trinity Sounds, King Tobby, Mao Anbassa Sounds and Foundation International. The 1980s produced many more sounds, and it brought with it the decline of the Sound System Movement, as Black community radio came on the air, and provided the same type of well-loved Black music for many thousands of people at one go. This aspect of the Sound System Movement and Black Radio will be looked at in Volume Two (1976-95) of this work.

The influence of the sound system was total in the African Caribbean Community. Sounds provided entertainment at christening, birthday parties, engagements, weddings, anniversaries and at wakes. Sound system entertainment was the main type of entertainment for the African Caribbean Community.

The music to which the immigrants were accustomed in the Caribbean - Calypso, Ska, Bluebeat, Rocksteady, and later Reggae and Soca, were not available in England. They were sent from Jamaica and Trinidad to relatives and friends living in England. Immigrants coming over might bring recently released records. Others were sent through the post.

A sound system social function could attract hundreds of guests, particularly when they had access to the local town halls. The scarcity of venue for Black entertainment in England guaranteed success of sound system functions. To add extra excitement, well-known and popular 'sounds' compete for the 'best sound' title. This sort of function could gather at least fifteen hundred people, most of whom were youngsters, in their teens and early twenties.

The Black Sound System Movement was particularly important to Black record producers in the Caribbean, particularly in Jamaica, Trinidad and Tobago and Barbados. Without the Sound System Movement,

Caribbean home-grown artists could not be heard in England. White pop music was hardly played on the BBC, let alone Caribbean, Africa and Asian music, in the 1950s and 60s, until BBC was re-organised, bringing about Radio One and local BBC radio stations. American Black Jazz artists had their music aired on British radio and later Television. More Black images were seen on British television as soul music became popular - *Top Of The Pops* TV Programme, *Opportunity Knocks,* with Hughie Greaves, among others, gave exposure to multi-cultural pop artists and new talents, like Birmingham born, young Lenny Henry, whose parents were Africans, born in Jamaica.

Later people like Cy Grant, Trinidadian singer, and the Oxford educated Ian Hall, born in Guyana, Director of Music, at the London University, presented *Songs That Matter*, in 1972, a regular sing along popular type of songs on Sunday afternoons transmitted by Associated Television, which was based in Birmingham.

Sound system was famous for their 'blues', 'shebeens' and basement parties. This type of social functions brought the operators in conflict with the police, partly because of neighbours' complaints about 'loud music'. Some neighbours were not satisfied with complaints, they took direct action, as was recorded by the *'Black Voice':* [1]" On 3rd January, 1971, over 100 Black people were in a party at Sunderland Road, Forest Hill, London SE23, when, at about 1.30am, the house was petrol bombed by four White youth. Over 30 people were injured, including Mrs Cherry Jackson, Cathy Renford, Leroy Jackson and James Fuller, all people of African origins, who suffered third degree burns. The Police arrested and charged three youth with 'arson' and 'setting fire to a dwelling house'

---

[1] Black Voice Volume 2. No.1Page 5. Published by BUFP, London 1971

Sound systems were self-financing, which might be owned by one person or members of a group. Group ownership meant in some cases that one person purchased records regularly to keep up with other sounds, another purchase the amplifiers, including pre-amps, and another purchase the speaker boxes. Another system might be based on a 'collective' where members of a group pooled their finances and purchased what was necessary to keep the Sound going. One member 'chat' - what might be termed a Master of Ceremonies (MC) in the formal sense, but dynamic and artistic; and one select the records to play - 'the Selector'. There would have been other secondary helpers. Many youth liked to be seen with a sound system. A very successful Sound Group might own a medium sized van to transport the sound equipment - speakers, amplifiers and wires, records, sound (speaker) boxes and helpers to 'lift' - carry - the sound boxes.

Some sound systems were sponsored by record producers in the Caribbean. Many sounds took on 'colonial' names - like 'Duke', 'Count', 'Sir', and so on, largely satirical statements, reminding the astute supporters of their struggles for their rights of passage. It was a tradition passed on by Marcus Mosiah Garvey, the Pan-Africanist, who argued that Black people must have their own titles, as they choose.

This is not to say that Sound men aspired to a 'Black Aristocracy'. It was a symbolic reminder to all concerned that while Black people were being oppressed for the time being, that situation was rapidly coming to an end. Repression did not obliterate the great heritage of the African, and that heritage lived within, and some day, it would again manifest itself extensively overtly for the good of humanity.

The Black Sound System Movement in Britain, therefore, guaranteed good home made entertainment. It created cultural self-sufficiency. It secured the cultural identity of the immigrants, in the face of racism, which attempted to commit cultural genocide, with the full recognition that, if you cut the roots of a tree, it would die.

While this is not a study of the Black Sound System Movement in Britain, it is a demonstration of a way in which an oppressed people responded to current social conditions and maintained their own cultural norms in order to conquer the   silent swell of institutionalised racism. Sound system owners were ordinary men, who demonstrated Black grassroots credentials.

Let us therefore *salute members of* Britain's Black Sound System Movement   - those of the past, present and those who might come, in whatever form, in the future. The Sound System brought a type of unity in diversity to the Black Community in Britain, during the 1950s, 60s and 70s.

Like Black book shops, it was necessary to set up Black music/record shops. One of the very early Black record shops were Slim Pecking, Gangsterville, Burning Sound and the Palmer Brothers, who moved on to setting up 'Jet Star' Records Distributors. Later Players were Hawkeye. While 'Trojan' were supplying records to the Black Community, Black ownership was uncertain. Black people from the provinces often came to London, the Capital City, for their supply of Black music.

Jazz music was still having a revival during the 1950s, 60s and 70s. This type of music was particularly popular with Middle class Britain, and Black American artists were in demand. These records could be purchased in Caucasian owned record shops. While the immigrants liked Jazz music, and listened to it intensely, it was not the majority's first choice. Soul music was on the horizon, which eventually captured the hearts and minds of both Black and White youths, given the advent of

Rock 'n' Roll with Chubby Checkers, Fats Domino and others.

Black Gospel music was popular among the religious and partly religious members of the West Indian Immigrant Community. Members of the emerging Black-led churches had a demand for this type of music. Gospel music was played in many West Indian homes during Sundays on the family best.

In Bristol, Sylvester Eugene, born in Jamaica, was a freelance promoter for up-and-coming amateur Black artists in the area. He also arranged social functions at the local Community Centre and at *The Bamboo Club*, that was owned by Tony Balimore, a member of the Jewish Community. Most of the artists who appeared at *The Bamboo Club* were Black. Benny E. King, a famous American Black Soul Singer, appeared. Prince Brown, Jamaican born, was one of the local MC at *The Bamboo*, whose job was to put on stage, amateur as well as professional artists. That was his pride and joy.

Claude Brooks, born in Anguella, the Leaward Islands, Caribbean, and based in Slough, Berkshire, set up his Claude Brooks Entertainment Agency in 1968. One of his first clients was 'Tropic Isles' a band which specialised in calypso music. Claude Brooks became famous after his band appeared on the Hughie Greaves Show, *Opportunity Knocks*, in 1968. From them on, the Agency went from strength to strength, through the 1960s, 70s, and beyond.

However, the really popular artists came from Jamaica and Trinidad. They were brought over - a way of saying that they were under contract to individuals, as opposed to big entertainment agencies. That was an attempt by members of the Black Community to keep ownership of Black music and culture. In the early years, many contracts between artists and individual promoters were verbal.

Both the artists and promoters took the risks. The promoters would pay the artist's air fares, hire the venue, print the flyers - publicity materials, distribute them as widely as possible and hope for the best. Some events succeeded. Other did not.

With the introduction of commercial Black newspapers, like *The Westindian World,* and other specialist music paper with an interest in Black music, like *The Black Echo, Black ownership was uncertain, and Melody Maker,* this gave Black music promoters access to a larger audience which they did not have before. This encouraged record shops generally to stock Black music for commercial motives.

This opened the way for the vast commercialisation of Soul Music in the late and mid sixties. Motown Music, with Diana Ross, Stevie Wonder, The Jackson Five, Otis Reading, James Brown, Marvin Gaye, Tina Turner, and many more, lifted the spirit of Black people in Britian to a new level of pride. The White Left began to set up music radio and broadcast on the high seas, like Radio Caroline and Radio London, with Tony Blackburn, Caucasian, and others. Over fifty percent of their round-the-clock music, beamed to Britain, were by Black - African American and African Caribbean artists'. The British public - the young particularly, asked for more and more. White Britannia began to dance and shake her hips to the rhythm of African culture. That Culture had, and continue to have, unprecedented influences on White Britain.

Black music gave birth to major White bands like The Beatles, Rolling Stones, The Who, The Small Faces, and other British bands. The same type of influences were felt in the USA and elsewhere.

That was potentially big business, which drew the attention of the Establishment's entrepreneurs, who wanted a piece of the action. BBC was re-organised and commercial radio licences were issued to members of the White Community. Capital Radio in London came on air in the early 1970s. BBC tried to compete with local commercial radio by opening up local radio stations across Britain. The flag ship to this BBC experiment was BBC Radio London. A commercial demand for Black music was created, which caused the Black Music Industry to expand. Members of the White Community were posed to make a fortune from Black Culture, and that they did.

Bob Marley, the Jamaican Reggae Artist, who was growing into a Giant, was eventually selected by Black and White record buyers as the torch bearer of reggae music. Sparrow in Trinidad was the King of Calypso.

Green Sleeves Records And Island Records in Britain, White owned, appeared and cut deep into Black culture and profited at the same depth. Black up-and-coming artists were gathered, in England and the Caribbean, graded, some selected, promoted and managed by another culture. Black music was on its way to be colonised.

By the mid 1970s, Caucasian promoters were signing up as many young Black signing talents in London. They were tied up for at least two years. Black youth did not understand the game of which they were made a player. That type of mass signing, as it were, guaranteed the silence of many talented Black singers for at least two years.

That type of blanket signing, eliminates presented no potential competition to the Caucasian promoters. The promoter had no real intention to bring the majority of the newly acquired young Black artists in the recording studios, let alone putting them on stage. The cream of the Black talents were acquired and exploited. The colonisation of Black culture by Caucasians had began in a big way.

Black culture was carrying the swing in substance. Great White Groups like the Beatles, Rolling Stones and others, subsequently openly declared that their concept and application of music was based on Black artists and their music.

The White working glass and middle class were gyrating to Black music. This made it a little more difficult for racists to argue that Black people were uncultured. Black music brought friends from the White Community. African culture as it evolved in its modern setting under the strains of racism, which emanated from the depth of the African psyche, as existed in the African Deoxyribonucleic acid, DNA, for many thousands of years. That made the racists looked foolish, as their children - sons and daughters, brothers, sisters, uncles, aunts, grand mothers, fathers, cousins, nephews and nieces, showed publicly their appreciation of Black Culture.

The explosion of Black Culture created greater confidence in the minds of the Black settlers in Britain during the 1970s, as *Culture*, a greater force, took up the fight to maintain Black people's identity.

The conditions were created for more young Black writers to emerge, bringing with them new talents, which Britain was yet to experience. Robert Birmingham, born in Aruba, in the Caribbean, and Donald Kinch, born in Barbados, were young writers with vision during the mid

1960s and the 1970s. Birmingham set up The Black Writers Association and Kinch, the Staunch Poets And Players. Because of the initiatives of both Black writers, they provided platforms for old and new writers to meet and perform their works, at a time when those platforms were needed to build confidence in young Black people. Both groups were based in West London.

The West Indian Students during the 1960s and 70s made important contributions to the up-liftment of members of the Black Community in Britain. In London, the central venue for West Indian students' activities was 1 Collingham Gardens, Earls Court, London SW5, in the London Borough of Kensington and Chelsea.

The Centre was maintained by Caribbean governments for West Indian students on government grant aid or scholarships to Britain, who were expected to return to the Caribbean after their studies. This idea of returning might not have been rigidly applied.

At the front, advocating for Black rights, was the Poet and Novelist, Rudolph Kizerman, born in Barbados, previously known as Rudolph Brathwaite. He inspired many with his book *'Stand Up In The World'.*

The Centre provided an invaluable platform for free expression. There was no similar centre in London, either for members of the West Indian Community or West Indian Students. The core leadership of the West Indian Students' Union (WISU) during 1969-71, called on their government to open the centre to members of the West Indian community, in view of the scarcity of meeting places in London and elsewhere. The record showed that the Centre was never formally given over to the wider West Indian Community in Britain.

The formal position made no difference because the wider West Indian Community used the Centre anyway to call meetings with the support of the WISU. Gary Burton was born in Antique, a law student and President of the WISU. Ansel Wong was born in Trinidad, a student of English And American studies, and Chairman of the WISU. These two men played pivotal roles in facilitating positive activities at the WISC. Other West Indian students took what appeared to them the easy option and buried their heads in the bosom of non-activities, which in themselves appeased racism. If there was no resistance to racism, racism won.

During the UNITY WEEK in August, 1969, organised by the West Indian Students and held at the WISC, Andrew Salkey, writer, broadcaster and playwright, born in Colon, Panama and a Jamaican citizen, remarked: "If our community does not exercise its will to achieve the very ordinary base of identity and trust it will never realise its aspiration towards an effective political opposition in a xenophobic and racialist society."

Eduard Mondlane, said about Africa and the concept of civilisation,: "The Concept of 'assimilation' is not as non-racial and liberal as its apologists suggest. It involves no acceptance of the African as an African...he must live in an entirely European style; he must never use his own language, and he must not visit unassimilated relatives in their own homes...the most that the *assimilado* system ever sets out to do is to create a few honorary whites, and this certainly does not constitute non-racialism.'"

Chris Lemaitre, born in Trinidad, was a leading figure in the West Indian. Student Centre Legal Panel and active in the work of serving the cause of Black people in Britain. His fight against exploitation dated to the early 1960s.

To assist in maintaining collective identity, Errol Lloyd, a young Jamaican Painter and Sculptor, was dedicated to ensure that the identity of the African people in Britain was not eroded. Some of his work adorned the Main Lounge of the WISC, including portraits of George Padmore, Pan Africanist, born in Trinidad, Marcus Mosiah Garvey, Pan Africanist, born in Jamaica, and a bust of C.L.R. James, Writer and Philosopher, born in Trinidad.

Three years later between 26 June to 15 July, 1972, Errol Lloyd put on a major Exhibition of paintings and sketches at the Ecumenical Centre, Denbigh Road, in Notting Hill, West London. His 74 exhibits of African images, most of his own work, made an important statement about Black images in an environment which was overtly racist and hostile to members of the Black Community.

Gary Burton showed strong and passionate leadership of members of the Union in 1969, as he reminded members, during the UNITY WEEK, that: "unity is absolutely essential. We must be strong, united and fighting for a common goal - *OUR SECOND EMANICIPATION."* [Emphasis is his.]

Some of Ansel Wong's contributions to Black identity was his writings and directing plays at the Centre's Black Art Workshop, which he founded. The Workshop also performed plays by other Black writers.

Ron Karenga summed up the themes of the Black Arts Workshop: "We have always said...that the battle we are waging now is the battle for the minds of Black people, and that, if we lose this battle, we cannot win the violent one. It becomes very important then, that art plays the role that it should play in Black survival and not bog itself down in the meaningless madness of the Western World. In order to avoid this madness, Black artist and those who wish to be artist must accept the fact that what is needed is an aesthetic, a Black aesthetic, that is a criteria for judging the validity and/or the beauty of a work of art."

Radical Poets like Faustine Charles, born in Grenada, Horace M. Lashley, born in Trinidad, Jamil Ali, born in Guyana, and June C. Doeley, born in Jamaica, used the WISC, with its ready audience, to introduce their work. June C. Doeley had considerable talents as a poetess, telling in frightful symbols and forthright images of Black Experience. She was a member of the Black Arts Workshop and Vice-President of the WISU.

With the introduction of a Trinidad style Carnival in Notting Hill, the organisers gave steelbands a new and urgent meaning in England. One of the leading lights in getting the steel band accepted as an important art form, was Selwyn Baptiste, born in Trinidad. To do that, Baptise and his colleagues of the Adventure Steelband, began the process of educating members of the public about the history of the steelband. That was their role at the UNITY WEEK at the WISC.

In focussing on the role of the steel pan, Patrick Griffiths, born in Trinidad, said: "...the steelpan projected from a sub-culture and continue to exist on the same socio-cultural level...the rhythms of the steel-pan projected the excitement-factor embedded in our psyches - closer to the emotional spirited - worship heritage...of energy/involvement/wonder....the steel-pan: a historical artistic instrumental expression, completely unique - the symbol of an origin"

Clarence Thompson, born in Trinidad, poet, demonstrated that the fire for Black identity was burning fiercely in his belly, during the 1960s and 70s, as shown in his work - "Portrait Of A People". In "Ballad Of A Slave" he lamented - "AFRICA ! AFRICA! AFRICA ! Oh Sweet Africa ! A child of your womb awaits the hangman's noose. I stand here caged and shackle".

Clarence Thompson, later became the General Secretary of the West Indian Standing Conference, expressed the anger felt by members of the African Caribbean Community in Britain during the 1960s and 70s .

Linton Kwesi Johnson, born in Jamaica, published his "Voice Of The Living And The Dead" in 1974. Johnson introduced his unique style of 'dud' poetry to Britain, which captured the imagination of the young. Dub poetry is music and words in motion, that is, the Poets read as their words surfed the rhythms of the accompanying music.

On the question of sports, cricket was the premier leisure time activities for most West Indians during the 1950s, 60s and 70s. The West Indian Cricket Team were World Cricket Champions and they got full backing when they came to Britain, to play England in test cricket. Later members of the West Indian Community set up their own amateur cricket teams and joined local cricket leagues organised within the West Indian Community. Members of the Asian Community also set up their own cricket teams, clubs and leagues.

Local authorities' parks were hired during the summer for cricket matches. The parks were also used for football games, during the winter months.

At most Caribbean social centres in London, Manchester, Liverpool, Preston, Birmingham, Bristol, and where a community centre might be hired, including church halls, domino games were some of the main indoor sport. Domino games were also played at home, if a centre was not available.

West Indians took their domino playing to an art form. They organised domino tournaments - competitions, among themselves at various parts of the country. That was also an opportunity for the family to have a day out. Coaches would be laid on.

Boxing was the other sport which interest almost all members of the West Indian family. The great sports men of the boxing world during the 1960s, like Sonny Liston, Joe Frazer, Muhammad Ali, George Foreman and Britain's home grown John Conteh from Liverpool, brought many hours of enjoyable entertainment to members of the community. Ali was most inspiring and brought pride to a down trodden people

As the children of immigrants grew up, they turned their primary interests to Soccer. They were to became some of Britain's best players. At first they were refused entry to White managed clubs, but they could not be excluded for long, as they demonstrated real skills on the football fields during practise matches and amateur competitions.

Sports were important media used by members of the Black Community to maintain their collective pride and identity in Britain.

Members of the Black Community in Britain, particularly people of African origins, began to read more.
There were popular secular writers who were widely read. Some of these were:

> Edward Brathwaite, born in Trinidad, *'The Folk-Culture Of The Slave In Jamaica',* Fidel Castro, born in Cuba, *'History Will Absolve Me';* Che Guevara, born in Cuba, *'Episodes Of A Revolutionary War';* George Padmore, born in Trinidad, *'Africa And World Peace',* (1937); Walter Rodney, born in Guyana, *'West Africa And The Atlantic Slave Trade';* Frank John, born in Trinidad, *'Black Songs';* Franz Fanon, born in

Martinique, in the Caribbean, *'Black Skin White Mask'* and *'The Wretched OF The Earth'*, (1965); F.O. Shyllon, *'Black Slaves In Britain'*, (IRR 1974); J.A. Rogers, born in the USA, *'World Great Men Of Colour'*; Bernad Coard, born in Jamaica, *'How The West Indian Child Is Made Educationally Sub-Normal In The British School System'*, (1971, New Beacon books); Arthur Ashe, born in USA, *'The Arthur Ashe Story: Diary Of A Tennis Star'*; C.L.R. James, born in Trinidad, *'The Black Jacobins'*; Angela Davis, born in USA, *'An Autobiography' (1975);* Martin Luther King, Jr., born in the USA, *'Why We Can't Wait' (1963);* Dilip Hero, born in India, *'Black British, White British'*, (1973); Nkrumah Kwame, born in Ghana, West Africa, *'neo-colonialism: The Last Stage Of Imperialism'* (1965); Marcus Mosiah Garvey, born in Jamaica, *' The Philosophy Of Marcus Garvey'*; W.E. DuBois, born in the USA, *'Black Africanism And Nationalism In West Africa'* And *'The Experience In Bondage: The First 300 Years'* (1975); Mao Tse-tung, born in China, *'The Thoughts Of Chairman Mao';* Huey P. Newton, born in the USA, *'Revolutionary Suicide'*, (1975); Eldride Cleaver, born in the USA, *'Soul On Ice'*; Rap Brown, born in the USA, *'Die Nigger Die'* (1969); Vince Hines, born in Jamaica, *'Britain, The Black Man And The Future'* And *'Black Youth And The Survival Game In Britain';* Eric Williams, born in Trinidad, *'Capitalism And Slavery'* And *' From Columbus To Castro';* Alex Healey, born in the USA, *'The Autobiography of Malcolm X';* James Baldwin, born in the USA, *'Go Tell It On The Mountain'* And *'The Fire Next Time';* Elijah Muhammad, born in the USA, *The Message To The Blackman'* And *'How To Eat To Live'*.

The Radical Alliance of Poets And Players (R.A.P.P.) made its appearance in 1973 to present 'roots' community theatre. The impact of their work was soon recognised and in April 1974 their musical narrative of Jamil Ali's play "Black Feet In The Snow" was televised on "Open Door" (BBC2). R.A.P.P. was re-formed in 1975 by a quartet of founder members: Shango Baku, Hausa, Adjewa and Khafre, who, as writers, actors, poets and musicians, continued on an extension of their original ideas of creating grassroots entertainment through music, poetry and movement. Their multi-talent blending brought a new form of Black Art expression to a United Kingdom audience as the Group tour colleges, universities and open spaces, including public parks, during the summer.[1]

Except for Dilip Hiro, Fidel Castro, Che Guevara and Mao Tse Tung, all the other writers and players were of African origins, conscious of their place in history and the contributions they must make to bring about fundamental changes in order to place the African back at the pinnacle of world leadership. Each dutifully made their contributions accordingly.

Roy Sawh, an Indian born in Guyana, South America, made a powerful contribution to Black civil rights in Britain during the 1960s and 70s. His was a face and voice heard at Speakers' Corner, in Hyde Park, London, nearly every Sunday afternoons, during the Summer, particularly from 1965-75. His 'free speech' forums attracted thousands of people over the period, many of whom were visitors to Britain and settlers, both Black and White people of various

---

[1] 'Dem A Come' - Patrick Griffith, Published by Radical Alliance of Poets And Players, London 1978.

cultures. Roy had a very quick mind and sharp tough, and were able to stand up to the most articulate heckler and debate subjects from the unjust war in Vietnam, racism in Britain, homelessness and youth unemployment, politics and many more.

Roy Sawh was an inspiration to many who heard him speak. He was a voice of defiance, in face of the culture of injustice that had existed at the time. He was one of the prime movers of creating a 'street university' in Notting Hill, West London - something of an open university, a similar idea of which was later introduced by the Establishment, with the creation of Britain's first Open University on air.

Amon Saba Saakana (previously known as Sebastian Clarke), born in Trinidad, was at the cutting edge of community advocacy for Black arts and culture. Based in Ladbroke Grove, Notting Hill, West London, Saba published the magazines 'Spirit' and 'Sun Song' - a book of Caribbean writers' poetry, in 1970. Through Saba's journalism, 1969-79, unknown Black artists were given exposures both in the Black and White press. Saba later went on to establish one of the Black Community's successful publishing houses - Karnak House in 1979, publishing African writers like Cheikh Anta Diop, Dr Charles Finch, Dr Jacob Carruthers, Dr Theophlle Obenga, Prof. Yosef Ben-Jochannan and Dr Chukwunyere Kamalu.

233

18. Birth Of The Black Media In Britain: 1945-1975

Marcus Mosiah Garvey's Newspaper, *The Blackman,* was the forerunner for people of African descendants. A liberation medium in the Caribbean, USA, Europe and Africa. *The Blackman* was published in the 1930s and circulated to over six million members of the Negro Improvement Conservation Association, usually called the Universal Negro Improvement Association or the UNIA.

Such an International Black Newspaper would have been circulated chiefly to students in Britain, mostly in London, Birmingham, Manchester and Edinburgh, Scotland, in addition to Black merchant seamen. That was because there had been very few Black people in Britain during the 1930s, which included diplomats, tourists and students.

The United States of America was the base of the UNIA, Marcus Mosiah Garvey and *The Blackman,* until 1935. Garvey transferred the headquarters of his Movement to   Hammersmith and Fulham, South West London. Garvey, Jamaican born and Pan-Africanist, died in London on 20 June, 1940.

Eighteen years later (1958), Claudia Jones, Trinidadian born and a socialist, who resided in the USA for a number of years, arrived in Britain and founded and edited the political newspaper, *West Indian Gazette,* which championed the cause of the arriving working class West Indian immigrants. With that sort of support, the new comers felt least isolated in England. *The West Indian Gazette* remained in publication until 1965. Its founder and editor died in 1964.

The *New Africa* Magazine was published in 1960 and edited by Mukhtar Mustapha. Another magazine was called *Africa*, glossy and rich in details. Both *New Africa* and *Africa* focussed on activities on the Continent of Africa. Most of their readers were Africans and African Students born in, or recently arrived in Britain from, the Continent of Africa.

In 1967, *The Hustler* was published, which was jointly edited by Courtney Tulloch, born in Jamaica, and Naseem Khan, born in India. *The Hustler* was based in Labroke Grove, West London and was the forerunner in mirroring the aspirations of urban Black youth, their love and hate of contemporary White Britain. *The Hustler* ceased publication shortly after its early circulation.

Theo. Campbell, Jamaican born, introduced and edited his Magazine, *The Jaffa* in 1968. That Magazine reflected the socio-economic life of the West Indians and encouraged business development. The Jaffa ceased publication during the early 1970s.

YOUTH FORCES FOR NATIONAL LIBERATION (YFNL) JOURNAL was first published in North London October, 1968. The publication had a stencilled format of 7x2 pages on both sides. Its editorial position was based on Maoist bias and, though published in North London, it targeted West Indian students, particularly the Jamaicans who were expected to complete their studies and return and make important changes in Jamaican society.

It is difficult to assess the level of its circulation. It was self-help, which gave radical voice to members of the Black Community. The unusual nature of YFNL was that it appeared to have been well-informed. Issue3, page3, published a full list of the number of 'enemy planes' shot down over North Vietnam, a total of 3,243 between 1964 and 1968; and the number of ships and boats sunk or damaged, including the U.S.S. Maddox, and that was 143 of the same period. It gave USA troops movement in Vietnam from January to June 1968, including the numbers killed.

Almost four months later, in Issue No. 6 April, 1969, price 3d, the publication carried a full statement by "Comrade Mao Tse-Tung, Chairman of The Central Committee Of The Communist Party Of China, In Support Of The Afro-American Struggle Against Violent Repression (April 16, 1968". The Statement was in connection with the assassination of Rev. Dr. Martin Luther King Jr.

What was unusual about YFNL was the quality of it information, providing up-dates of events at various parts of the world -West Indies, reporting on individual Islands, China, Vietnam, Laos, Albania, Palestine, Mozambique, Angola, Guinea (BISSAU) and Latin-America. The appearance of the publication was quite a low profile printing quality - in foolscap format, duplicating paper and hand stapled together. It was not a Broad sheet. None of the other grassroots publications at the period demonstrated such consistent qualitative information as YFNL.

There was a mailing address for articles and comments. According to YFNL, readers should *"read, distribute and discuss this Journal…The enemy is sharpening his sword and we, too, are sharpening ours ! …In Unity lies our liberation"*
After Issue 8 in June 1969, no more copies were to be found in the archives.

By July, 1970, The *Black Voice* was founded by the Black Unity And Freedom Party (BUFP), based in South East London. The *Black Voice* was an A4 format selling for one shilling (1/-) (5p), and was "set up to encourage and publish the peoples ideas and correspondence." Its primary aims were "to agitate, educate and organise black working people in the spirit of socialism and internationalism". Quotes were taken from *The Black Voice* inaugural publication Vol.1 No.1. *The Black Voice* was still being published in 1975.

Here it should be noted that many of the early Black Community publications were issued irregularly. Some were monthly, others quarterly and some weekly. Never daily. Publication happened when cash was in hand. Some were published without dates. Date of publications were sometimes identified by advertisement carried or recorded dates of incidents being reported on at the time.

The *Freedom News was* published by the British Black Panther News Service in 1969 which carried the message of the Black Panthers Movement. *Freedom News* was reported to have been edited by Althea Jones (Later called Althea Jones-Lecointe), born in Trinidad and later became one of the Mangrove 9 Old Bailey Trial. *Freedom News* had a national circulation among its members in the Black Community, distributed freely, paid for by members donations and voluntary work. Most readers of *Freedom News* were young people who had their personal experiences of police mal-practices on the streets, discriminations in jobs and housing, plus a 'generation' gap which they had to work out with parents. *Freedom News* ceased in the mid 1970s at the demised of the American Black Panther Movement, on which the British Black Panther Movement was based.

Flambeau - meaning a Torch, first published in Labroke Grove, West London, in January 1971, which carried a 5p price tag. It was published three monthly, by Grove Youth Group, some of whom were members of the local Metro Youth Club, and local residents. It was edited by Darcus Awusu, published under the name "Black Patch"

Flambeau ceased publication during 1971, at the end of the Mangrove 9 Trial.

During its publication, *Flambeau* exposed the repression of the local police in Notting Hill Gate. It also informed members of the public about events at the Portnal Road Demonstration on 9th August, 1970, which resulted in the Mangrove 9 Trial in the Autumn of 1971, and exposed the contradictions of the proposed Immigration Bill due to become law in August 1971. *Flambeau* reported on national conferences and demonstrations, and took a pragmatic approach to Black Community development. *Flambeau* had wide circulation, some copies were also circulated in the English provinces, where there was a high concentration of people of African origins, who were having common repressive experiences as those in the Capital City, London.

TriContinental Outpost[34] was a radical broad sheet published and edited by Ajoy Shankar Ghose, Indian born, which took up the civil liberty issue and focused specifically on the Black Conscious Movement. Its publishing slogan was - "Voice Of The Grass Roots. *TriContinental* was a 'monthly' Newsletter. By 30th October, 1970, 12 issues had been published with a price tag of 1/- (One shilling Stirling) . That Newsletter was associated with the local multi-racial 'Peoples Association', a Forum to exchange frank ideas. However, *TriContinental* was independent of all groups. Ghose was firmly in the driving seat. The Newsletter had a local circulation. After Issue 15 in February, 1971, *TriContinental* was not seen again. *TriContinental* invited its readers to 'open the mind' and 'Never judge a man on his skin colour, judge him by his conscious deed' - The Editor attributed that saying to Malcolm X.

As members of the Black Community experienced greater social pressures in England, they formed organisations appropriate for their defence. Each organisation developed its own news sheet of some sort, in order to get their messages across to members of the public and to keep their members informed of relevant information.

The *Grassroots* was first published in January 1971 as the Newspaper of the newly formed Black Liberation And Freedom Party, with its base in North London. *Grassroots,* published monthly, maintained a militant defence of members of the Black Community. It had been fearless in its challenges of injustices and racism. One of *Grassroots* aims was "to seek justice for black people". Tony Soares, Editor of *Grassroots,* appeared in court and received jail sentences for articles *reproduced* in *Grassroots.* The paper was in the frontline of fighting for human and civil rights. *Grassroots* continued publications into the late 1980s.

UHURU (freedom) and *UJAMAA* (nationhood) were both A4 stencilled reproductions and published between the late 1960s and early 1970s. Their messages were firm and clear, which held their own among the published Black Community based broad sheets at the time.

Both productions were youth managed, with strong afrocentric bias. 'Uhuru' was the freedom cry of the Kenyan MAU MAU Land and Freedom Army, which was launched in 1952 against British colonialism, and led by Dedan Kimathi. Ujamaa was Tanzania's slogan for African Socialism. *UJAMAA* members interpretation was 'nationhood'.

Both publications produced articles which sought to educate their young readers to their important link to Africa. Many young readers would have had Caribbean parentage, many of whom had not come to terms with their Africaness.

Both publications had strong Rastafarian influences and Black consciousness. MAKAKA (Basil Javis, Trinidad born, and one of the Inner London Education Authority's (ILEA) first youth workers) edited *UJAMAA).*

UJAMAA was also the Newsletter of the Youth Group, Universal Black-Peoples Improvement Organisation (UBIO), which was set up to "bring power and peace to all Black children in the country and others," accordingly to one of *UJAMAA*'s editorial. The Newsletter was given away free to its members and friends and paid for by members and friends subscriptions and donations.

UHURU was based in Peckam, South East London which was also paid for by members and friends, the publication was handed to members of the public for free. UHURU was the voice of Black People Freedom Movement, a British urban creation.

Both UJAMAA and UHURU were significant because they appealed to and got the participation of Black youth on the streets, who had very little understanding of polemics. They were searching for their identity living in a predominantly White racist, and in many ways, hostile England. Some youth were born in England, others came from the Caribbean to join families and became disillusioned. The publications were not pushing any political ideology - from the left or from the right. They were about raising awareness, self-esteem, a sense of pride, purpose, and social consciousness. Both publication succeeded . They got the support of their young readers.

The Abeng was launched in 1969 and catered chiefly for Caribbean students, particularly those from Jamaica and Trinidad. Its theme was based on socialist revolution in the Caribbean, given the example of Castro's Cuba at the time. There was no clear association with any particular party or group. John LaRose, of New Beacon

Books Ltd, was one of the leading lights of that Paper. *Abeng* was financed by voluntary donation. From an appeal made by the West Indian Student Union (UK) in July, 1969, which said, 'ABENG[1] is in need of your financial support. Please give generously to the Abeng Fund.'

Abeng's financial situation did not curtail its voice on behalf of members of the Black Community, as it stated in June of 1969: "Our identity with black people everywhere is not just a matter of sentiment or culture. Identity and unity with the black struggle everywhere is essential for the success of our own struggle - for our survival. The military arsenal of the white power structure is formidable for any one country, except Vietnam. But it cannot stop a revolution of black people in Jamaica, in Africa, in the rest of the Caribbean, in Detroit, in Chicago, in Alabama, and in Brazil all at the same time."

There was a commercial market developing in the Black Community for a national commercial weekly Black-owned and managed newspaper. In 1971, the *West Indian World* filled that gap. It was owned by Aubrey Baynes, born in St Vincent, in the Caribbean. The first Deputy Editor of the *West Indian World* was Lionel Morrison, South African born Journalist, of Zulu ancestry, who made important contributions to the development of the newspaper.

The *West Indian World* was first based in West London and subsequently moved to North London, and Arif Ali, Guyanese born, was appointed Editor. The *West Indian World* brought a different sort of voice to Black Britain. It had no real rival in the commercial field in providing community and international news to its readers. The *West Indian World* became a major black publication in

---

[1] UNITY -THE TIME IS NOW. West Indian Student Union Magazine, page 14. July, 1968, London

Britain between 1971-1980, and was well supported by members of the Black Community. It also attracted sponsorship from local authorities and central government in the form of full page job advertisements.

West Indian World adopted a non-party political approach. It presented the news in a factual way, and gave editorial support to any political party which appeared to be supporting the interest of the Black Community. It was fearless in fighting racism and often had some of its advertisements withdrawn because of it's firm stance against racism, xenophobia and religious intolerance

The *West Indian World* was a spring board for young writers, journalists, photographers, artists, etc. Some of those were Mike Philips, Guyanese born, Vince Hines, Jamaican born, Russell Pierre, Trinidad born, Neil Kenlock, Tony Douglas, Jamaican born, Caudley George, St Vincentian born, Arvil Smith And Dennis Morris, both Jamaican born, Hal Austin, Barbadian born, Louis Chase, Barbarian born, Devon Gordon, Stephen Bulgin, of African origins, naming only a very few. The average age group of the people mentioned above was twenty three.

While the majority of the *West Indian World* readers were Black, it was not exclusively so. The newspaper was published by Lenmond Publishing Ltd. The paper continued publication until the mid 1980s. It carried a £0.10p weekly price tag.

The *West Indian Digest* began publication on April,1971, and edited by Arif Ali. Its normal print run was 10,000 copies. The magazine was widely read through library and organisations, doctors' surgeries and clubs, as well as through subscription and sales in news agents. Its readership were 80% West Indians, 10% Asians, 8% Africans and 2% Whites and others. The *West Indian*

Digest circulation and reader profile were almost similar to that of the *West Indian World*. The Magazine was published monthly and cost £0.25p per copy.

Both publications were purely commercial which respected the intelligence and cultures of the readers. The *West Indian Digest* carried the following motto on each of its publication at the time: *"It's better to light even a little candle, than sit alone in the darkness."* The magazine was published by Hansib publications Ltd, which was still being published during 1975.

The Gleaner Newspaper, published by The Gleaner Publishing Company, Kingston, Jamaica, West Indies, was introduced in England during the 1970s. Most of the coverage of The Cleaner, focused on events in Jamaica. The Paper was not, therefore, qualified as a self-help initiative in Britain. *The Gleaner* did, however, provide an important service to Jamaicans, the largest group of immigrants from the Caribbean, living in Britain.

The Vanguard, published for the Oilfield Workers' Trade Union by The Vanguard Publishing Co. Ltd in San Fernando, Trinidad, West Indies, was also introduced in England during the 1970, and, like the Cleaner Newspaper, was not qualify in the study as a British Black self-help initiative. Nevertheless, *The Vanguard* provided import information to lift the spirit of Caribbean people in England, who were fighting racism, particularly those who came from Trinidad.

Black Liberator, a socialist oriented magazine made its welcome appearance in the early 1970s. The magazine was edited by Ricky Cambridge, Guyanese born, and a committed community activist for civil rights and anti-racism. The *Black Liberator*, in one of its issues, supported the Cuban Revolution as an important Caribbean event, during the 1960s. The Editorial Team devoted an entire issue of the *Black Liberator* by publishing the Cuban Government Five Year Programme. The *Black Liberator* was one of the first bulky Black quarterly magazines which stopped publication in the mid 1970s.

Race Today, founded by 'Towards Racial Justice' a church group, during the late 1960s, came under the management of *Race Today Collective,* nearing the middle of *the 1970*s. Leila Hassan and Darcus Howe, Editor, were some of *Race Collective* members. *Race Today* Collective's views were based firmly on socialist principles and the magazine gave its readers clear direction along those line. The magazine looked at issues in the Caribbean, the Americas, Asia, Africa, and Europe and championed workers' rights.

Colin Barker of the International Socialism said of *Race Today* in 1974, *"For reportage of the racial situation in Britain, Race Today is simply unequalled. The paper is lively, open and controversial. Every socialist should read it and use it."* C.L.R. James said *" In posing the revolutionary potential of Caribbean and Asian peoples. The new RACE TODAY takes a distinctive place in British journalism."*

There was no radio station, film company or television station owned or managed by members of the Black Community in Britain, between 1945 and 1975. Members of the Black Community were wholly dependent on the Black-managed press to be fully informed of events in their own Community at home and abroad. A struggle without its publicity organ was one unlikely to progress very far.

It was demonstrated that it was not the gloss and glitter which made a good successful media. It was clearly substance and the commitment of those who operated them. A thirsty person will drink clean water from any vessel, and if necessary he/she would get down and lap.

The thirst of Black people in Britain during the 1950s, 60s and 70s for self-awareness, which would hopefully lead to mental liberation, was satisfied to a large extent by the Black media at the time, which was managed by the grassroots for the entire people. There was no class barrier or ageism in reporting the news. A wide cross section of the community was served.

If Britain did nothing else, she allowed the freedom of the press, the Black Press, in spite of some serious harassment of the individuals who were closely associated with that Press, such as Tony Soares of *Grassroots* and others.

Others might argue that the British authorities did not 'allow' the operation of the Black Press, but the Black Press allowed its own operation. If it was not done openly, it would probably have gone underground, and so permission was not sought, and would not be sought from the very same people the evidence had shown to be engaging in a devious form of repression of members of the Black Community, particularly their young. What appeared to have saved the day, was the British Judiciary at the higher level, and some fair-minded and public spirited citizens, who served notice, to whom it may concern, that they were not prepared to play the racism game, but treat all accused justly. On appeal, a significant number of charges brought by the police against members of the Black Community were thrown out by the High Courts, most of the charges of which were dubbed 'political', by members of the African and Caribbean Community,

Unfortunately, some members of the Irish Community were not accorded that type of judicial objectivity at the time. A catalogue of innocent Irish men and women were changed by the police with monstrous crimes, including the bombing of public houses and killings in the process. Many were convicted, sentenced and served long prison terms, up to sixteen years in jail in some instances, before their innocence came to the public notice, and they were released.

The Irish and Black people social conditions were linked closely in British social history, particularly after 1948 ? *"No Irish"; "No Coloured", "No Dogs".* Both groups suffered almost similar social discriminations, except for colour. The reason for that link cannot be answered here. It might be a subject for a research undertaking.

John LaRose, born in Trinidad, supported by his wife Sarah, Caucasian, launched New Beacon Books in 1966. The name 'New Beacon' was chosen in light of the tradition of the Caribbean choosing light in publications: 'Origenes' in Cuba; 'Revue Indigène' in Haiti; 'Tropiques' in Martinique; 'Kyk-over-al' in Guyana; 'Bin' in Barbados; 'Beacon' in Trinidad; 'Focus' in Jamaica.

John LaRose explained in 1968:[35]
"New Beacon is an attempt to end the constant hiatus in certain areas of Caribbean life; to end the imprisonment in English, in Spanish, in French, in Dutch which accordingly denies areas of experience which, if made available, would immediately disclose the total specificity of Caribbean life; and to make each new generation aware that they are not starting from scratch...More autonomous appreciation of the World through publishing is what is needed. We have only taken a small step."

The other of Britain's early Black publishing house was formed in 1969, by Jessica Huntly and Eric Huntly, wife and husband team, born in Guyana. The Company took its name from two important figures of African struggle in the Caribbean - Paul Bogle born a slave in Jamaica in 1820 and led the Morant Bay rebellion in 1865. He died with 436 of his fellow fighters as the British Colonial masters asserted their control. Toussaint L'Ouverture, born in San Dominique (later re-named by the freed African, Haiti), led the 18th century slave insurrection in San Dominique and defeated the English, French and Spanish in battle.

The Huntlys therefore combined the symbolism of African resistance and called their new Company *"Bogle L'Ouverture Publications".* Their first title was Dr Walter Rodney's "Grounding With My Brothers". Other title by the same author was "How Europe Underdeveloped Africa". By 1975, *Bogle L'Ouverture Publications Ltd* published several titles written by Caribbean writers, including children books and English born young Black writers, like Accabre Huntley's 'At School Today'. 'How Europe Underdeveloped Africa' was translated in other languages - Portuguese, German and Spanish. Other writers were - Andrew Salkey, Kwesi Johnson, Phyllis and Bernard Coard, Accabre Huntley and Odette Thomas, both born in England, of African origins.

Zulu Publications was introduced in 1971 and published a number of titles, including *Britain, The Black Man And The Future, Black Youth And The Survival In Britain and A Movement For Change* authored by Vince Hines.

As stated elsewhere in this book, Black Radio and Television were non-existence between 1945 and 1975 in Britain.

Harrace Ovè, born in Trinidad and lived in Britain, a Caribbean film maker, extended his film making repertoire in 1970 and made a one hour long film, on Reggae. That was added to his two previous films, one on James Baldwin, African-American celebrated writer and Dick Gregory, African American celebrated comic.

"*'Pressure'* was Britain's first black feature film"[3] said Derek Malcolm, film critic of the Manchester Guardian Newspaper. Showed in 1974 and premiered at the 1975 London Film Festival. *Pressure* received success at film festivals abroad, winning silver medals at the 1976 Carifesta, the best Actress and Best All Round Picture. Pressure subsequently took awards at the 1977 Jamaican National Film Festival and invited to show at Chicago, Toronto and Festac, the Nigerian Black Arts Festival.

'Pressure' was Horace Ovè's debut as a feature film director.   Robert Buckle was the producer, and the eminent novelist, Samuel Selvon wrote the screenplay. The lead role was played by Herbert Norville. *Pressure* was shot entirely on location in London, and set in the 1970s at the height of the Black Consciousness Movement in London, as seen through the eyes of two Black youth. Other actors included: Oscar James, Frank Singuineau, Lucita Lijertwood, Sheila Scott-Wilkinson and Norman Beaton. *Pressure*   was A British Film Institute Film and released by Crawford Films Ltd.

Leaflets, flyers, wall posters, at A5, A4 and A3 single sheet format were simple and the most effective means of communication to members of the community during the 1960s and 70s. That medium was easy to put together, cheap, and easy to distribute. Any one with access to a duplicator could prepare and run off thousands of that type of publication.

They were used to inform members of the public about meetings, demonstrations, police incidents that happened in the Black Community, dances, including concerts, parties, christenings, weddings and deaths.

These leaflets and flyers were distributed to selected members of the public at bus termini, tube and railway stations. Wall posters were past up at strategic locations, normally at nights to avoid prosecutions for bill sticking.

The Chinese had been using wall posters for years to inform members of the public of current events of interest. That was particularly successful in Chairman Mao Tes-ting Red Guard China,[37]during the middle of the 1960s

The White owned and controlled media showed no real interest in catering for members of the Black Community at any level. The exception to that was the British Communist Party's, Morning Star Newspaper, the Socialist Worker and the Manchester Guardian. In 1968, the BBC Television in its *'Cause For Concern'* series documented an eye opening account of police corruption and brutality against Britain's Black Community. Derek Humphry, Caucasian, born in England and a senior reporter on the Sunday Times,[1] brought to the attention of his readers, from time to time, the racism being experienced by members of the Black Community.

The White Left was generally supported of the Black Conscious Movement during the 1960 and 70s. At the same time there had been a 'Flower Power Movement' with the slogan - "Make Love Not War", young Whites rebelling against the *status quo.* The injustices of the Vietnam War were points of focus for White youth to air their protests. White underground newspapers like 'Ink', which was edited by John Lloyd, supported by Dave Robins, and Judy Groove. *'International Times'*, Edited by Paul Louis, *'Oz',* Edited by Felix Dennis, *'Time Out',* *'Release'* and *'Gay News'* carried articles exposing racism in Britain. Dave Turner designed anti-racist

---

[1] Derek Humpry And Gus John Sunday Times Article, page 6, 30 August, 1970, London.

posters for anti-racist demonstrations, with his distinctive trade mark - a large red arrow.

The Socialists were still optimistic of a Socialist World Order and Black people were the visible evidence of exploitation and repression world wide. Linking with Black struggle gave the White Left the necessary credibility they needed - evidence that they were involved in a practical grassroots struggle for change in the *status quo.*

The White Left recognised that the ownership of Black leadership must remain with the Black Community, and not with the Whites. If members of the Black Community needed any specific support, the White left was available.

With that policy, Black and White activists were able to work together to challenge racism, xenophobia, homophobia, sexism, anti-Semitism and religious intolerance. In the early part of 1971, a National Demonstration was called against the 1971 Immigrant Bill which was to become Law in August of the same year.

During the demonstration, the White Left marched behind the banner of the International Socialist And Communist Party, the Asians, behind the banner of the Indian Workers Association and the African/Caribbean behind the banner of the Black Conscious Movement. They marched together under the slogan *"BLACK AND WHITE UNITE AND FIGHT"* and "KILL THE BILL ". The immigration Act was passed into law the same year.

The White Left provided media tools to members of the Black Community, like printing press, duplicators, art work studios and type-set facilities at reasonable costs. Many members of the White Left were young Jewish activists.

Most members of the Black Community could not identify a Jewish person from any other member of the White population, neither did they seek to make such an identification, as there was no relevance. However, years later, it came to the author's attention that many of his closest working colleagues and activists, particularly in the field of journalism and broadcasting, were members of the Jewish Community, who were in the front line of ensuring that the Black Community's was heard in the media where possible. Those friendships survived the sands of time. That is not to say that all members of the Jewish Community were supportive of Black peoples liberation.

The 1960s and 70s type of civil rights movement are likely to be needed again in Britain, appropriately adjusted to reflect the culture of the current state of society. The subtle but rising tide of racism, xenophobia, anti-Semitism and religious intolerance remains potent. In respect of the Police/Black Community relationships, during 1987 and 1997 there had been a steady growth of Black people dying in police custody, without anyone brought to book. At the last count in summer of 1997, a total of ten Africans - some born in the Caribbean and others in Africa, died in suspicious circumstances, while in police custody.

In addition, a number of Britain's policy makers who seemed to lack vision are trying to manipulate and direct Black-managed voluntary and community groups, with the co-operation of a well-placed unrepresentative minority, members of the Black Community. The apparent manipulators seem to be using funding, grant making and financial donations, as means of social controls. Inadequate resources from the public purse is offered for vital core support of Black-managed voluntary and community services. In addition, the High Street banks are still slow in offering high risk venture capital for African and Caribbean business development in Britain.

As for Black-managed voluntary and community sector, the little resources on offer, are offered on a *'stop and go'* basis, particularly to national *representative* Black strategic community development organisations. That type of *'funding to fail'* strategy, guaranteed at best, the control of growth, and at worst, nil growth of the groups concerned. Black leadership aspirations for the wider Black Community are therefore frustrated.

To function in the current state, the African, African-Caribbean and other visible minority communities are thrown on a dependency existence, which leads to Black leadership made to appear weak and inadequate. On the face of it, those members of the Black Community, who are exhibited by the *status quo* as 'making it' - and often partners to empty rhetoric, are invariably those individuals and groups who sip with *Injustice* and betrayed the universal order of *Natural Justice* and members of the poor and dispossessed. Britain's Black communities do not need minimal patch work social, economic and political successes, but significant collective community development, which can be replicated by *any* section of society.

There is a rising level of poverty in Britain, both for black skin and white skin citizens. Black people and other people who experienced injustices of any sort, must build and maintain a culture of resistance to any and every policy which deprived social justice. A resistance which cuts across class, gender, colour, creed and age.

Those funders who are guilty of creating obstructive machinery - with the hope of dictating the pace of Black Community development in Britain and elsewhere - must think again. It is far better to create policies for harmonious community relations   rather than social controls. British History   clearly demonstrated that a policy of social control invariably back-fire, at a time that it was least expected.

The birth of the British Labour Movement was partly the result of a failed policy of social controls of the White working class in Britain during the 19th Century. Members of the Black Community are the synthesis on which Britain should build for the future. White Britain or Black Britain will not be able to put the clock back. The winds of change are already with us and have become a storm. If we resist it, we are likely to be floored as it is with powerful natural storms, which devastate objects in the way - trees, houses, bridges, towers, men and beasts.

While there exist fundamental social injustices in society, Black people will be true to their experiences, and respond appropriately, within a liberal democracy, such as Britain's. That democracy will only work effectively, if it works for all, as citizens exercised their rights under the law,   resisting social, economic and political repression, in its subtle modern forms.

The historical certainty is that members of the Black Community will resist injustices of all types - they have a very long history of doing that, and they will not stop now. They are a people of *Natural Justice* and they will settle for nothing less.

As we saw in the former Yugoslavian State, Bosnia and Serbia, during the 1990s, human intolerance was only surface deep, ready to raise its head at any time. Vigilance and alertness must always be the order of the day, to all civilised thinking people, whatever their politics, gender, creed, culture, colour of skin or sexual orientation. Ignorance must be kept firmly chained at the edges of oblivion. NOBODY WINS THE RACE WAR !

The Black Media in Britain served members of our multi-cultural society well, without which Britain could well have become a wilderness of racial bigots and bigotry. White Britain must not forget to say occasionally - *'thank you Black Britain'.*

The Challenge now is for the Black Community to establish a firm presence on the World Wide Web - the INTERNET. We must be a core part of the cutting edge of modern technology, on earth and in space. Our leadership role therein must be second to none.

19. The Emergence Of National Non-Party Political Black Community Development Organisations 1959-1975

BY 1959 Britain had a well-developed Voluntary Sector. Some of the known names at the time were: Women Voluntary Services (WVS), the Red Cross, The Salvation Army, the Boys Brigade, The Boys Scout and Girls Guides, The National Council For Voluntary Organisations, The British Association Of Settlements And Social Action (BASSAC), London Voluntary Service Council, the National Association For The Care And Rehabilitation Of Offenders (NACRO), the National Society For The Prevention Of Cruelty TO Children, Dr Barnados Homes, naming only a few of the household names.

These groups catered mostly for, and managed by, White skin people. Black skin people hardly had a look in, either by service provision, employment or management. If any did, it would have been the exception.

Barnados Homes catered for a significant number of bi-racial, crudely called 'half-caste' children, often abandoned by their parents, normally Caucasian women, who had been abandoned by their Black male partners. It was a very brave 'black and white' couple who stayed together and raised a family in view of the racist, name calling environment in Britain, during the 1950s, 60s and early 70s. That bravery did exist.

A number of children, born of African couples, most of whom were students from West Africa, were found in the Barnados homes. The students could not cope with their studies and bringing up their children at the same time. As a result, children grew up in homes without their natural parents. To many students, that situation was a temporary one, as they intended to take their children back to Africa after they finished their studies, which could last up to five to seven years. As a result, many of those children grew to adulthood without a sense of identity and lost contact with their ancestral African family.

There had been cases where West African students, having completed their studies successfully and ready to return home with their children, faced refusal by the authorities, on the grounds that the children would be better off brought up in Britain. The courts often supported that line, particularly when the child was placed in foster care for a long time.

The idea of a Voluntary Sector was unknown to the incoming immigrants from the Caribbean, Asia and Africa. Those from the Caribbean, and some parts of Africa, knew about the Salvation Army. The new comer did not think that they would need the services of voluntary groups in Britain. The immigrants were strong and healthy and came to work, make enough money and return home, 'after five years'. That was the general plan.

Moreover, immigrants would have been used to getting help, when necessary from their extended family. However, the racism which Black people experienced on arrival in Britain, threatened their security and sense of identity, and they began to form associations. That was a new experience to many members of the immigrant community, particularly those from the Caribbean.

The Hindu, Buddhist, Muslim and Sikh were used to a 'structured' form of living as their religions required. After physical emancipation from British slavery, in 1838, the

Africans in the Caribbean ensured that they lived largely easy-going lives. They valued freedom. The Africans in the West Indies choice of religion were largely influenced by the White missionaries. The Africans from the Caribbean could not practice openly any other religion except Christianity.

When they could, the Africans exercised a wide variety of choices within the Christian Faith - Anglican (Church of England), Baptist, Methodist, Roman Catholic, Seventh Day Adventist, Jehovah Witness, Pentecostal and later Ethiopian Orthodox Church (Rasta). The Indians and Chinese were allowed to practice their own religions - Hindu, Buddhist, Islam, Sikh or none at all. They were allowed to keep their own languages as well. Not so with the Africans in the Caribbean.

The Jews, some of whose ancestors were the primary force in underwriting the Slave Trade[1] from Africa, retained their religion, language and influence in the Caribbean. The Africans were not converted to Judaism. West African who came directly from Africa to Britain during the 1950s, 60s and 70s had a mixture of religions - Traditional, Islam and Christianity.

The Africans from the Caribbean, therefore, were best placed to assimilate in British religious life, since they were taught by the British missionaries that 'we are all equal before God'.

With that in their minds travelling to England, the Africans from the West Indies did not plan to create

---

[1] For further details on this fact, refer to the work of Sons Of Liberty, 'Who Brought The Slaves To America', Carnegie Institute of Technology, Pittsburgh, Pennsylvania, USA. This revelation sometimes surprised many modern citizens. We should remember, however, that the slave trade was big business, and anyone with a desire to make more money during the 17th to 19th century might have been tempted to invest in this trade, including ship owners and insurance brokers, except for the Quakers who wanted to have nothing to do with enslaving the Great African People. Our knowing the facts should help the healing process.

groups exclusively for themselves, as they would have preferred to join existing social, religious and other British institutions.

Social hostilities against the Black immigrants did not allow that type of social and religious mix in any significant way. In view of the relative social rejections by White Britain, the immigrants were forced to consider setting up their own secular and religious institutions. Their first call was to form religious denominations - free churches.

Most of the immigrants from the Caribbean were religious, not all wanted to go to church. They wanted social and recreational centres which offered culturally sensitive activities.

There was a proliferation of nationals associations. The Indian Workers Association (IWA) had its origins in the social and cultural cohesiveness of the Punjabi community, during the 1950s and early 60s. Most of the Asian immigrants settled in Southall, Leicester, Derby and the industrial centres of the Midlands, most of whom came from the Jullunder and Hoshiarpur districts of the Punjab.

IWA started as a cultural and social meeting place for Indian immigrant workers, as a focus of nostalgia and national pride. Later, IWA became political in face of the Labour Party immigration laws in the late 1960s and unfair treatment of IWA members in the factories[2].

The Immigrants from the West Indies formed their own associations, representing members from Jamaica, Trinidad and Tobago, Barbados, Grenada, Guyana, St. Kitts, St. Lucia, Leeward Isles, Antigua, St. Vincent and

---

[2] New Perspective On The Asian Struggle. Part 2. Race Today Collective. Volume 11. No.4. November/December, 1979, p104. London

Monsserrat, and from Africa - Nigeria and Ghana, and from Hong Kong, Chinese groups, most of whom could be found in Manchester and Central London. Later associations were formed to represent those from newly independent Pakistan and Bangladesh. Unlike the IWA, most of these nationals associations remained non-political.

Many of the nationals associations became members of local co-ordinating committees, like the West Indian Co-ordinating Committee, which was set up in Manchester in 1966, based at the West Indian Centre, Carmor Road, Chorlton-on-Medlock, and represented all the West Indian nationals organisations in the area. That was local co-ordination. In Liverpool , also in 1966, similar arrangements were made with the Merseyside Caribbean Council. In Preston during the mid 1970s, the Preston West Indian Centre was opened to accommodate the local West Indian nationals groups.

Partly because of a serious threat from racist thugs on the streets and the overt racism from the wider society, the West Indian Standing Conference (WISC) was formed in 1959 as a national response to racism and repression against the West Indian people in Britain. WISC was a representative non-party political advocacy Forum. WISC accepted membership from individuals and associations. Between 1959 and 1969, WISC was the premier national organisation in Britain, which advocated on behalf of members of the West Indian Community.

WISC did not set up hostels, nurseries for the under fives, supplementary schools, youth clubs or community centres. That was not the role of WISC. Other Black-managed groups were beginning to do that type of work at local grassroots level .

Between 1964 and 1974, there was a strong Black Consciousness Movement in Britain. People stopped calling themselves 'coloured', and 'brown' as euphemisms to 'black' . They now called themselves 'Black' - if they looked black or of African origins. Some Indians began to call themselves 'Black' some said 'Brown'. Many talked in terms of 'Black' and 'Asians'. That type of self-description sometimes confused some people. To those of African origins, 'Black' was for collective convenience, and 'African' described Nationhood, in Africa and the African Diaspora. The Chinese remained Chinese.

Britain's Black Conscious Movement focussed on civil rights issues, particularly members of the Black Community experiences of repression at the hands of the police. In Britain, that Movement was fuelled by the American Civil Rights activities, led by the Black Panther Movement, whose leading lights were Bobby Seale and Huey P. Newton. Other influences were The Nation of Islam, whose leading lights were Honourable Elijah Muhammad and Malcolm X El Hadji Malik El Shabazz (Malcolm Little), the Student Non-violent Co-ordinating Committee (SNCC) and its leading light Stokely Carmical (Kwame Ture), and the Southern Christian Leadership Conference, leading light, Reverend Dr Martin Luther King Jr.

By 1971, Britain's Black activists began to focus their activities on practical community development programmes to help the poor at the grassroots, and high profile rhetoric became secondary, if at all.

Many new groups were formed, in 1975, whose management wanted a new type of local, regional and national representation. These included hostels, community centres, youth clubs, advice agencies, housing co-operatives and sports clubs. The official Race Relations Movement - which came about with the

1965 and 1968 Race Relations Acts - to be reinforced further by the 1976 Race Relations Act - started to compete with the traditional leadership of the immigrant community, for the attention of members of the Back Community. That was the start of the substantive weakening and duplication of the independent representation of Black people in Britain, which contributed to the eventual split of the African and Asian Communities.

A three day Conference[1] of Black People in Britain was called in London on 17,18 and 19 January, 1975.

The idea of the Conference sprang from a realisation that the proposed Forum on race in the UK funded by the Calouste Gulbenkian Foundation and sponsored jointly by the Community Relations Commission and the United Kingdom (Geneva) Division of Social Affairs, should be preceded by an opportunity for a representative group of Black people to come together to express their views on important and neglected racial issues of the day as they saw them.

At the National Conference a resolution was passed recommending the abandonment of the Forum and a National Association of African, Asian, and West Indian organisations as proposed instead. The Conference wanted the continuance of a Black/White dialogue.

The Conference believed that there was:
   1. "A dire and long standing need for Black people in this country to be afforded an opportunity amongst themselves to express their point of view, their concern, opinion and general experience in relation to policies/programme produced by a host

---

[1] 'Black People In Britain: The Way Forward'. Leaflet published in London in 1975 by Post Conference Constituent Committee

community that condones racist discriminatory legislation, and rather paternalistic programmes. They have a clear perception of their contribution in this society but must be allowed to define their own problem, solutions and priorities.

2. "A need for a new organisation, the members of which must represent the people drawn from grass root organisations of the Black community including those persons who suffer discrimination on grounds of race, colour, ethnic or national origins and not just officially sponsored bodies so that a new organisation concerned with the affairs of the Black community be under the control of elected representatives of the Black community"

The Conference also "resolved to form a National Organisation of Black People in order to unite their efforts to combat racial discrimination and work towards the realisation of equal opportunities for Black people". Deputation presented evidence and values to Mr Alex Lyon, then Minister of State, Home Office, the Select Committee on Race Relations and Immigration, and Mr Roy Jenkins, the Home Secretary.

The January 1975 Conference passed another resolution that 'a committee consisting of the Chairman, Speakers, and Rapporteurs of plenary sessions and sub-groups, together with Conference Assessors and Conference Joint Secretary should be mandated to carry out the resolutions passed at the conference and keep watch over developing race relations legislation".

The following were members of the Committee:

Oscar Abrams, Dr. A.K. Admani, S.I.Aziz, Jocelyn Barrow, Professor Thomas Blair, Dilbagh Chana, Dr. Rajeev Dhavan, Stuart Hall, Professor A.G. Hines, Mrs K.K. Khan, Surendra Kumar, Charles J. Mungo, Syed Safirunddin, Dr A.F.A. Sayeed, Phil A.C. Sealy, Vishnu Sharma and Peter Tucker.' The Committee appointed Dilbagh Chana and Hal Austin as Organiser/Fieldworker and Fieldworker on a short-term basis.

Nearly all of the above named were born in the British colonies in India (parts of which were later called Pakistan and Bangladesh) Africa and the West Indies, including Guyana. Thomas Blair was a USA citizen, working at one of the British education institutions in London.

Within a year, nothing became of the Conference and it faded away. The Black grassroots did not have ownership of the initiative. The people who were being harassed on the streets and experienced real racists attacks did not support the Conference, partly because they did not know about it and the people who originated it.

The conference organisers were not the people whom members of the Black Community saw taking risks on their behalf on the front line of street protests, at marches against racial harassment and police brutality.

The Conference appointees were not the people who were being arrested and threatened with long prison sentences in British jails, in the name of Black civil rights.

The new Community Relations Commission (CRC) and its surrogates, local community relations councils, were being used to sap the energies of independent Black initiatives. There had been no real effort by members of the Establishment - who were behind the initiating of that Conference, to encourage an effective National

Black-managed Organisation to grow and provide a powerful democratic voice of the British Black dispossessed.

Vince Hines wrote a newspaper article, at the beginning of 1975, called 'A MOVEMENT FOR CHANGE', which was used later for the title of his third book, which suggested that there should be a national umbrella grassroots organisation for members' common interest, which would not discriminate on the grounds of race, class, gender, age, religious beliefs and practices, tribe, marital status, age, political beliefs or sexual orientation. The Organisation should be one, where there was no voting place for the individual membership.

On July 1975, The Vince Hines Foundation, a national registered education Charity based in West London, with the support of the Melting Pot Foundation, a registered charity, and the Brixton Neighbourhood Association, a registered charity, both based in South London, convened a general meeting in London, and gave birth to The National Federation of Self-Help Organisations (NFSHO).

The inaugural meeting elected Vince Hines, Trustee and representative of the Vince Hines Foundation, Chairman of the Central Committee, Mr Rene Webb, representative of the Melting Pot Foundation, General Secretary and Courtney Laws, Director and representative of the Brixton Neighbourhood Association, Honorary Treasurer. Other representatives were elected to serve on the Central Committee, and as regional representatives.

For the first time, the Black Community produced a *non-party* political national generalist independent non-governmental organisation, which was able to link grassroots members from Africa, the Caribbean and Asia in a common bond to fight racial discrimination and to help create better social conditions for members, with *Community development* as its primary objectives.

The special difference was that the Federation's membership was made up of organisations and not individuals. That was an important beginning for Britain's Black Voluntary Movement, which took on a professional approach to sustained Black community development.

The basic purpose of NFSHO at the time was to bring Black-managed groups together in conference and exchange ideas, make general policies for the Black Self-Help Movement, assist with organisation development, monitoring and evaluating of service delivery and advocate on behalf of members.

NFSHO members were voluntary and community organisations with charitable objects, multi-faiths, credit unions, community business, islands associations, youth groups, housing groups, women's groups, gay and lesbian groups, education groups, Saturday schools, books shops, art groups, hostels projects, Rasta groups, senior citizens groups, information and advice agencies, race relations groups, professional associations and co-operatives . NFSHO was non-party political, whose slogans were *'Self-Help Is The Key'* and *'Building Our Community Together'*.

NFSHO was to become the largest and longest serving Black-managed community development national umbrella organisation in Britain. The Federation developed over a twenty three year period, promoting Black community development, which cannot be addressed here, but in the second volume of this book - 1976-95, except to say that within ten years of its operations, the Federation was serving over two thousand Black self-help and community groups in England, Scotland and Wales. There has been no similar organisation operating in the Black Community to date.

For the first ten years of its inauguration, NFSHO was funded by voluntary workers and donations by its members. That gave the organisation the necessary independence to develop a culture of speaking fearlessly on behalf of its members, without bothering weather its funding would be cut by being seen as going too far in advocating for the poor and racially abused. It can be an hazardous task to advocate for the Black poor and disadvantaged in a relatively racist society. It can be equally hazardous to advocate for the White poor in a society whose sensitivity for the poor and socially vulnerable weakens daily.

The Federation received its greatest obstructions from members of the official Race Relations Movement. *The politics of envy and personality were always within easy reach.* The Black oppressed were not encouraged to develop viable and sustainable community development network, without hard struggles.

In addition, the Race Relations Movement had attracted some of the best brains of the Black Community. If these brains were allowed to enter business, Britain's Gross Domestic Product (GDP) would have been greatly improved. Many Black individuals, who are engaged in the official Race Relations Movement, have become disillusioned, and often murmur words of regrets, which question the continuance of the entire 'official racial equality' programme. Meanwhile, new buzz words surfaced - 'equal opportunities' and 'human rights'. *'Race'* was being removed from the Agenda.

REDISCOVERY
If you cut
The roots of a tree
It will die.

A People without
A knowledge of its *History*
Is a People
Without memory.

A People without
Its *Languages*
Is a People
Without speech.

A People without
An *understanding*
Of *Self*
Is a People
Unable to define
Its past
Present and future.

A People without
Direction is a
People vulnerable
At the mercy
Of predators, exploiters
Injustices and inequalities,
Groping in the
Dark

QUICKEN your pace
Of *Rediscovery*
You Mighty People.

THIS IS YOUR
TIME

Vince Hines

**The Liberation Of
The African Consciousness**

*Awake Africa,
Awake*

*Your Children bid
You Come forward*

*UNITE
Children of Africa*

*Receive the Glory of
Your African Ancestry,
Ascending into the
Light of Our Consciousness*

AFRICA, AFRICA !

AFRICA IS AWAKE !

Vince Hines

In The Next Volume

VOLUME TWO (1976-1995): *'HOW BLACK PEOPLE OVERCAME FIFTY YEARS OF REPRESSION IN BRITAIN: 1945-1995'* will consider The Development Of National Black Self-Help Organisations and The Growth Of Black Voluntary And Community Groups, Including Black Businesses 1976-95. The Politics of Funding Black Community Groups, 1976-95. Notting Hill Carnival And The Carnival Movement In Britain 1976-95. The Black Community And Self-Help Sporting Initiatives 1976-95. School Exclusions Of Black Children 1976-95. The Black Community And Health 1976-1995, Black Supplementary Education And Its Influences On Community Education, 1976-95. Black-Led Churches 1976-95. The Thatcher Era And Its Damages To The Black Community 1979-90. Youth Uprising And Street Riots, 1981-1995. Health And The Black Community In Britain, 1976-1995. Black Housing Associations Movement, 1985-1995, Black People And Death In Police Custody, 1976-95. How The Official Race Relations Movement Impacted On The Black Self-Help Movement 1976-1995, African And Asian Conference (UK) 1990. The Hopes Of The European Union And The Response Of Britain's Black Self-Help Movement, 1990-95.
Zulu Publication
March, 1998

Reference Notes

[1] Brook, J., Minority Groups Employment Project, London Business School. January, 1978

[2] Thompson, C.C., The Quest For Attaining Excellence In Education. Published by The African Caribbean Education Resource Centre, January, 1995

[3] Smith, A., MSc Thesis on Health Care For African Caribbean Over Sixties

[4] Walker, D., Cabinet Papers of 1954:1. Public Record Office at Kew. Published by The Times Newspaper, London. 2nd October, 1985

[5] Who's Educating Who ? The Black Education Movement And The Struggle For Power. Race Today Magazine, Volume 7. No. 8. PAGE 182. August, 1975

[6] Green, S., "Rachman". Hamlyn Paperbacks, London 1981/ Kirkpatrick, B., Rachman: Fact Or Fiction ? Review in THE URBAN INFORMER.. Issue No. 6. Vol. 1, pages 19-20. London 1981.

[7] Who Minds - A Study Of Working Mothers And Childminding In Ethnic Minority Communities. Published by Reference And Technical Services Division, Community Relations Commission, London 1975

[8] Reference Division. Unemployment And Homeless: A Report. Pages 46-47. Published by The Community Relations Commission . London HMSO 1974

[9] Demuth, C., 'Sus' A Report On The Vagrancy Act 1824 Published by Runnymede Trust 1978

[10] Makanji, N., and Addai-Sebo, A., 'GARVEY IN LONDON'. Capital Issues Supplement, pages 12-13.Published by The London Strategic Policy Unit, 1987

[11] African Liberation Day '96 -Commemoration Brochure. 'A Brief History Of African Liberation Day', pages 13-15. Published by The All African Peoples Revolutionary Party, London 1996.

[12] Powell, E., Freedom And Reality. Arrow Books, London 1968

[13] Race Today Collective. New Perspective On The Asian Struggle, Part 2. Race Today Magazine, Vol. 11 No. 4. pages 104-105, November/December, 1979, London

[14] Black People's News Service, page 8, Issue February, 1970 and page 4 Issue September, 1970. Published by The Black Panther Movement, London

[15] GRASSROOTS - Black Community News: Volume 4 No.3, page3 - 'What Is The BLF', 29 September, 1975. Published by The Black Liberation Front.

[16] BLACK VOICE. Issue August-September 1970. Page 4. BUFP Manifesto 26th July, 1970. Popular Paper Of Black Unity And Freedom Party, London.

[17] CAAP NEWSLETTER SUPPLEMENT. Issued 28 February, 1970, page 2 - A Reminder Of CAAP's Programme. Published by The Council For Afro-Asian Peoples, London

[18] Race Today Magazine Volume 8. No. 10. Pages 195-207. October 1976. Published by Race Today Collective, London

[19] RACE TODAY. Volume 7. No.8 August 1975, page 182 Black Community Fights Back. Published by Race Today Collective, London.

[20] Hines, V., Britain, The Black Man And The Future, page 16. Published by Zulu Publications, London, 1971 and 1972

[21] Oaks, R., THE FLAMBEAU No.2 3rd March, 1971, page 2. Published by Grove Youth, London

[22] Conference Report by The High Commissions of Jamaica, Trinidad And Tobago, Guyana, Barbados, Commissioners For The Eastern Caribbean Government And Central Committee of Police Federation of England And Wales, 28th November, 1970. Held At The Commonwealth Institute, London. Published by Laurence London, Jamaican High Commissioner, 48 Grosvenor Street, London W1X 0BJ.

[23] Hines, V., Britain, The Black Man And The Future, Mangrove 9 Court Report, pages 22-28. Published by Zulu Publications, London 1971 and 1972. Ink Newspaper, December, 1971, London

[24] Race Today Magazine. Volume 6 No. 4 April 1974 pages 167-173. Published by Towards Racial Justice, London

[25] Narayan, R., Black England - A Reply to Enoch Powell, page 1. Published by Doscarla Publications, London 1977

[27] Narayan, R., GRASSROOTS Newspaper Volume 4. No. 8 September-October, 1976. 'Cricklewood To Leeds -The Cross-Country Legal Conspiracy', London

[28] Wood, W., Keep The Faith Baby, pages 10-16. Published by The Bible Reading Fellowship, 1994

[29] Hines, V., Conversation With Michael Abdual Malik (Michael X) Recording At The Black House 27 July, 1970

[30] Brother Herman, Secretary. General Letter Addressed to 'Dear Brothers And Sisters' on BLACK HOUSE, Racial Adjustment Action Society Headed Paper, pages 1,2 and 3. 95-101 Holloway Road, London N7 21st May, 1970

[31] Dashiki Annual Report 1972/73. Published by The Dashiki Council, London. March, 1993

[32] ADVICE Brochure, September, 1970. Published by The Community Development Trust, London

[33] Stroude L., Profile: Courtney Laws. 'SELF-HELP NEWS' No10. Page5. July 1986. Published by The National Federation Of Self-Help Organisations (UK), London

[34] Ghose, A.S., Editor, Tricontinental Outpost, Voice Of The Grassroots. Newsletter Issues 12 And 15. Collator - A.S. Ghose, London 30th October, 1970/February, 1971

[36] Malcolm, D., WEST INDIAN WORLD Issue No. 343, page 4, 23rd February, 1978, London

[37] The Economic "The East Is Blood Red" Issue 6438, 14th January, 1967, page 100. Mao Tse-tung China and changes in 1967